I0456125

FOREWORD

"It is very dangerous to be Right,
when the Government is Wrong."
- Voltaire

Wake Up, America!

WAKE UP...WAKE UP...WAKE UP! The IRS-CID is outside of your door. You are away on business. Your wife, who is also a mother of six, is home alone with your youngest daughter, getting her ready for school. Without warning, two dozen heavily armed "Special Agents" of the IRS-CID (Criminal Investigation Division) break into your house surprising your wife and daughter. Almost all of the Special Agents are large men, heavily armed, with bulletproof vests on. There has been no warning. There has been no Notice of Deficiency, no Information Document Request, no notice of any audit, no audit summons, or any letters from the IRS questioning any tax return you or your family has ever filed. This true story was covered by most newspapers around the Country between April 13 and 16, 2010 (for example, see Boston.com for just one of the many stories; just search for Fort Wayne, Indiana IRS raid).

This is no mere violation of the Fourth Amendment of the Constitution of the United States. This is an armed commando raid on Americans – on United States citizens. The President was upset that a Boston police officer wrongfully arrested a Harvard professor who happened to be an African-American, and that "misunderstanding" led to beers in the Rose Garden of the White House. The Attorney General has written a book called *"A Nation of Cowards"* regarding race, but how does the Attorney General not investigate Special Agents that work for him that have violated fundamental laws of this Country?

Dear Reader, this book is written for you in the hope that it is not too late to save the Country from the road that it is currently on. You must vote Republican in these Congressional and Senate elections because if you don't, you just may become a victim of the President's new IRS-CID "wealth-squad" attacks, even if you are not wealthy. No warning – only a sealed search warrant based on lies or innuendo from your neighbors or business competitors or corrupt informants – a sealed warrant that will take you months or years to unseal. Don't think that it can happen to you? It happened to Senator Ted Stevens, the longest serving Republican Senator in the United States Senate. If the Government can raid a Senator's house without probable cause, how can you possibly be safe? The Attorney General was so shocked by the egregious prosecutorial misconduct against Senator Stevens that he made a motion to have all charges against him dropped. But the misconduct by the Government destroyed Senator Stevens' reputation and also his life. Senator Stevens, a great American, died of a broken heart in disgrace, with no chance to clear his name.

You are probably not a Senator though, and neither is your wife. You are a hard-working businessman that has applied for financial aid for your college-bound children. Your wife is a homemaker and mother of six, and you live in a middle class neighborhood in Fort

Wayne, Indiana. You do not live in Beverly Hills or in a New York City penthouse – there is absolutely nothing about your lifestyle that would lead anyone to believe you are fudging on your taxes or living beyond your means. But, even if you were cheating on your taxes, why did you not receive an audit notice? What was the reason for the armed commando raid on an innocent housewife and her daughter?

Armed commando raids like this were meant to be stopped by the Roth Hearings, the Webster Commission Task Force, and the passage of the IRS Restructuring and Reform Act of 1998. Attending the Roth Hearings on IRS abuse of the American Taxpayer, deceased New York Democratic Senator Daniel Moynihan was heard to say "My God, we must stop these armed commando raids on American citizens."

Congress did pass the necessary legislation to protect American citizens, and the Webster Commission Task Force was established to review whether the IRS-CID commandos were following the rules that the IRS had imposed on them. When the Government was sued years later in one particular *Bivens Action*, the IRS-CID agents testified that they could not even remember what the alleged "probable cause" was that required the armed commando raid in the first place rather than serving an administrative audit summons, subpoena, or even a search warrant in the "least intrusive means possible." (See IRS Manual – yes, the IRS's own rule book – Part 9.4.6.1). (A *"Bivens Action"* is named after and refers to a Supreme Court case, <u>Bivens v. Six Un-</u>

known <u>Federal Agents</u>, 403 U.S. 388 (1971), which allows for a civil tort claim against the Government and/or Government officials for violations of the Constitutional rights of citizens during one of these raids).

Do you expect the Courts to help save you? Forget about it. In all of those thousand page bills that Congress passed without reading, they put in provisions that allow the IRS to assess $200,000 penalties that can grow to over a million dollars. These penalties are not subject to any judicial review and can be imposed by any out-of-control Field Agent of the IRS.

And if you wanted to sue the Government, it is a very difficult thing to do. This is true even though the Supreme Court has taken away "qualified immunity" from the IRS commandos who do not follow the rules (see the IRS Manual Part 9). But in several hundred *"Bivens-type Actions"* brought against the IRS commandos to date, none were successful because the Courts always felt the "IRS must be right" or would say "I just cannot bring myself to find bad faith on the part of the Government."

As if that is not bad enough, once the innocent victims bring an action against the Government, the Government in turn then brings an action against them, tells the jury that this person committed tax fraud, and a totally innocent person spends four years in jail. If you don't believe it, see the case of Dr. Daniel Levito in which even Judge – now

Supreme Court Justice – Alito states that Dr. Levito was clearly a victim of a violation of the Fourth Amendment during a commando raid of his small veterinary clinic where the Agents sent away clients of the firm, sent the employees home, and ransacked his clinic. Because Dr. Levito had the gall to sue the Government, years later he would be indicted for tax evasion and his wife was given probation for testifying against her own husband because he was exercising his First Amendment rights in advocating a book on tax avoidance. It seems only fair – since the Government put him out of business as a veterinarian – that Dr. Levito became an anti-Government, anti-tax advocate. Some of the arguments that Dr. Levito and his partners make in "their" book are totally frivolous and the IRS now has a portion of their website dedicated to these "frivolous", if not borderline illegal tax evasion ideas. Those types of "frivolous" or "illegal" tax evasion arguments are nowhere to be found in this Book. In fact, every single tax saving idea mentioned in this Book can find support in the IRS's own Revenue Rulings, Regulations, Tax Court cases, and the IRS's own website.

The protections for the American Taxpayer are also found on the IRS's own website and in the IRS's own Manual, which is available online. The Webster Commission Report is available in PDF format online. Remember, William Webster was a former Judge and the head of the CIA, and even he was shocked by the level of Government abuse of innocent American taxpayers by the IRS-CID.

The reason for writing this Book is that we are genuinely frightened that the President wants to hire 16,000 new Special Agents who will engage in **Sealed** Search Warrant, secret, armed commando raids on innocent American citizens and businesses. We use the word "innocent" because in 90% of the armed commando raids, there is **no** later assessment of taxes. After a two year investigation following the raids that disrupted the business, there is no "crime" or even tax deficiency found that would have warranted the raid in the first place. Remember, this is the IRS-CID, not the FBI or Drug Enforcement Agency or Bureau of Alcohol, Tobacco & Firearms. So, instead of serving an audit summons or subpoena, they have several dozen armed commandos in Kevlar vests with IRS-CID printed on the front, executing a **sealed** search warrant that you will not see for several months to several years after you file a Rule 41(g) motion in order to get your property back and unseal the warrant and affidavit.

Did we mention the President wants to hire 16,000 new Special Agents for the IRS-CID just to do this sort of work? The Government will only hire 800 new SEC Agents to keep Wall Street in line. This, even after the Bernie Madoff debacle and Goldman Sachs paying a fine of only a half-billion dollars for helping to bring down the economies of the Western World with toxic mortgages. Notice that friends of Goldman convinced the Government to put in $200 billion to save AIG with $60 billion going directly to the coffers of Goldman Sachs from the AIG guarantee of bad mortgage bonds. Lehman Brothers was allowed to go under, while AIG was saved by the Government so it could make good on the guarantees that Goldman Sachs had hoped to exploit in creating the toxic subprime mortgage market in the first place. Goldman has not had to plead guilty to anything or even admit fault. The $550 million fine is two weeks of revenue for Goldman – a mere traffic ticket – relatively speaking. But the same Government that will fine doctors and other small businesses up to $800,000 for failing to report a "listed" or "reportable" transaction that they did not even know they had participated in, and this is four to five years after the small business had adopted an ordinary pension plan with life insurance in it, lets big Wall Street firms off the hook so that they can pay record bonuses to their executives two years in a row after allegedly the greatest financial crisis since the Depression. Of course, you cannot believe it, because you think this is America, and excessive penalties like that would violate the "excessive fines" clause of the Eighth Amendment, the "takings" clause of the Fifth Amendment, and even the "*ex post facto*" clause of the Constitution, because fines of this magnitude are clearly "punishments" and not traffic fines or ordinary civil penalties. But these "punishments" are meted out every day to small, unsuspecting businesses that do not have thousand-dollar-an-hour tax attorneys to defend them as does Wall Street.

The America that you grew up in is rapidly vanishing and being subsumed by an overly-intrusive Government whose uncontrolled spending is threatening your family's future financial prosperity, freedom, and in certain cases – your life. The $13 trillion current deficit and $70 trillion in unfunded future liabilities will either be handled by bankrupting America now or from the tears and loss of freedom by your children and grandchildren. The deficit will not go away by itself and the President has signaled that he will hire 16,000 new IRS-CID Special Agents who will break the law with armed commando raids into the homes and businesses of innocent American citizens. Nothing like this has happened in this Country since British troops would routinely break into the homes of Boston housewives while their husbands were at work in order to demand money to pay for an out of touch, out of control, and overly intrusive Government in England. Make no mistake: no one in Washington cares about you. If they would raid a United States Senator's home, indict him on totally bogus charges, and find him guilty through egregious prosecutorial misconduct, then you have no hope of being safe. Instead of passing the Dodd-Franks banking reform bill, Congress could have instead reinstated the Glass-Steagall Act, which served us well for 70 years. The same is true with the "up-tick rule" to stop the relentless shorting of stock by greedy and well-connected Hedge Funds, almost all of whom have accounts or friends at Goldman Sachs.

You, unfortunately, probably do not have a clue as to what we are talking about, or how this will negatively affect your future, because no one from the Government has pointed out to you all of the terrible things hidden in all of these thousand page legislative acts that no one read. Even at this late date, you ask your candidate for the Senate or Congress how they feel about abortion, the death penalty, gay marriage, or gun control issues (issues which members of Congress could not control even if they wanted to). Washington is squandering your resources and the Nation's resources at an unprecedented rate. You must vote Republican in this election so America can return to its greatest years of 1994-2000 when we had an intelligent progressive-liberal President in the White House with a Republican Congress filled with deficit-hawks that did not care what anyone did behind closed doors.

Rest assured, if you do not vote Republican in 2010, your doors will eventually be kicked down by an out of control IRS-CID that must find more and more tax revenue through fear and intimidation just to **pay the interest** on our national debt. Forget the principal or future entitlement programs, just the interest on our National debt will take up our entire tax revenue when interest rates hit 6-7%. Because of a new Tax Code Section that was put in by the Healthcare Reform Bill – all transactions over $600 must be reported by **all** taxpayers, **even you**, no matter whether you are a Republican, Democrat, or Independent.

The Government is out of control and is dangerously close to be willing to sacrifice the future liberty and prosperity of its citizens on an altar of ever-growing deficit to fund an overly intrusive and invasive Government. It does not matter if the Speaker of the House is your best friend, or the Senate Leader is your father; the time is now for every voice to be heard before it is too late. There are some clarion voices that have been talking and writing about the decline of the American economy and the American way of life in the face of an ever-increasing Government that is out of touch with the American people. The list below is not meant to be overly expansive, and might exclude some names that deserve to be on it, but these are people who have done a good job in trying to change America and save the World and they are truly the "smartest guys in the room":

- Roger Ailes – Fox News
- Michael Bloomberg – Mayor of New York
- George H.W. Bush – 41st President
- John Kasich – Future Governor of Ohio
- Bill Clinton – 42nd President
- Jim Cramer – CNBC Talk Show Host
- Steve Forbes – Publisher
- Bill Gates – Philanthropist
- Sean Hannity – Author and Talk Show Host
- Larry Kudlow – CNBC Talk Show Host
- John McLaughlin – Talk Show Host
- Judge Napolitano – Author and Talk Show Host

- Bill O'Reilly – Author and Talk Show Host
- Joel Osteen – Pastor of the Lakewood Church
- Pete Peterson – Foundation Chairman and Author
- Mitt Romney – Former Massachusetts Governor
- Joe Scarborough – Author and Talk Show Host
- Rick Warren – Pastor of the Saddleback Church
- Mort Zuckerman – Publisher

To find an example of what America will be like with another 16,000 Special Agents hired to invade innocent American businesses and homes, one need look no further than Special Agent Shaun Schrader, who has no problem providing false information to a magistrate judge in order to get a **sealed** search warrant approved so that the armed commandos of the IRS-CID can raid an innocent business without giving them any warning. Special Agent Schrader is, in fact, famous for raiding popular restaurants at lunch hour, during their busiest time of day to make sure that you, patrons and proprietors alike, fear the power of the IRS. One restaurant he raided in Rochester, Minnesota was run by a local chef who had worked his way up from nothing to being one of the best known chefs in the state. Special Agent Schrader operates out of the Milwaukee IRS office, but he is known to travel all over the Country to tell lies about small businesses in order mislead the local magistrate judge into signing a **sealed** search warrant, so that the business will have no idea what is about to befall them. Special

Agent Schrader never follows the rules that are clearly outlined in Part 9 of the IRS's own Manual. See, e.g., IRS Manual Part 9.4.6 requiring the IRS to use the **least intrusive** method possible. Special Agent Schrader is exactly the sort of new irresponsible IRS-CID cowboy that you need to fear. He will tell any lie and state any misinformation to support his required affidavit to establish "probable cause" that there is some reason the unsuspecting business – the restaurant in this case – will destroy the evidence that the IRS needs to make their case against them.

Now let us assume, just for the sake of discussion, that this well-known restaurant in Minnesota really was keeping two sets of books. Is an armed commando raid with three or four dozen armed agents with bulletproof vests at **lunch time** really the "least intrusive" way to get that information? How about a raid at eight o'clock in the morning as the IRS-CID did in Fort Wayne to an unsuspecting wife and child? Or how about on a Saturday morning at ten o'clock, when no one ever goes to a restaurant? No: Special Agent Schrader wanted everyone in Minnesota to know this restaurant entrepreneur was suspected of tax fraud.

The only problem with that theory was that they never found the second set of books, or any tax fraud whatsoever. Especially in this day and age, when most people pay their bills at a restaurant with a credit card, wouldn't the "least intrusive manner" as required by the

IRS's own Manual be to execute a Third Party Summons on the credit card companies to get all of their payments from that particular restaurant? If the credit card receipts showed $3 million in gross income for the restaurant and the restaurant only reported $2 million or $1.5 million in revenues, then you have a case for tax fraud. What about expenses? The law already says that you must prove each and every deduction. In the future, you will need to report every expenditure over $600 as a small business, even for nondeductible expenditures – which was part of the Healthcare Bill that no Congressman read – and every business in America must justify and document every deduction that it puts on its tax return. Thus, if Special Agent Schrader feels the restaurant is "fudging" or "fiddling" on its taxes, why not issue an audit notice and make the restaurant prove each and every deduction as it is required to do under the tax law? The IRS never did that despite Special Agent Schrader's commando raid, and no tax fraud was ever found against the restauranteur even though his business was raided and his reputation forever tarnished. The family in Fort Wayne was not so lucky, however, and that is why we are writing this Book.

Jim and Denise Simon of Fort Wayne, Indiana received absolutely no warning that they were under investigation by the IRS or the IRS-CID. The agent in charge of the case, Special Agent Paul Muschell, wrote an affidavit to secure the **sealed** search warrant that has been described by professionals to be replete with numerous factual and legal errors, clear misrepresentations of both fact and law. Testimony by Special Agent Muschell appeared to the attorneys involved in the case to be designed to mislead the magistrate judge into granting the search warrant and to have it sealed. In other words, the same sort of affidavit that Special Agent Shaun Schrader might have done, complete with misinformation, misrepresentations, and misleading innuendo.

Neither Jim nor Denise Simon ever had any problems with the IRS in the past, and to this day, there has been no evidence presented that at the time of the illegal raid on the Simon's residence in Fort Wayne, Indiana, that Jim Simon had filed any false or even incorrect tax returns concerning his business affairs. Not only was there no probable cause for the search warrant or to have the search warrant **sealed**, there was absolutely no reason for the raid. Does an armed commando raid of two dozen husky Special Agents with weapons drawn, covered with bulletproof vests, shouting "IRS-CID" at a housewife and her 10-year-old daughter make any sense to you? The IRS, in its own Manual, instructs the IRS-CID officer in charge to use the "**least intrusive means**" of investigation available in all cases (see IRM Part 9.4.6.7.3.3).

When the storm troopers broke into the house of an American housewife – a mother of six – getting her youngest daughter ready for school, they accused her and her husband (who was overseas on business) with a multitude of crimes including tax evasion, fraud, money laundering, as well as other things that Denise Simon had no comprehension of and clearly did not believe or understand. The reason this is so painfully apparent is that within a few days of the raid, Denise took her own life as she was terrified by what had transpired in her family home.

The suicide letters she left behind to each of her six children and her husband are heart-breaking and can be found at www.rememberdenise.org, and at other sites on the Internet. We will only reprint here the general letter she left behind proclaiming her innocence, as well as her husband's innocence, of any and all crimes of which they were accused:

I am truly innocent of any attempt to evade taxes, launder money, commit fraud or any of the other things I am being accused of. I know of no attempt on Jim's part to willingly or knowingly evade taxes, launder money, commit fraud or any of the other things he is being accused of. However, I also have no faith in the legal system or the ability of the government to seek truth. I am currently a danger to my children. I am bringing armed officers into their home. I am compelled to distance myself from them for their safety. Being innocent is simply not enough for the government. – Denise Simon

With my dying breath, I swear Jim & I are innocent.

– Denise Simon

As one might expect, Mr. Simon's attorneys filed all sorts of motions under the Freedom of Information Act (FOIA) to find out what this was all about. His attorneys also filed many motions to unseal the **sealed** search warrant affidavit submitted by Special Agent Muschell. Surprisingly, once the Court unsealed the affidavit, there was no information there to let anyone know what the Simons were actually accused of, what crimes they had allegedly committed, or why some unarmed IRS agent in a suit and a tie could not have served the Simons by mail or even better, sent a Third Party Summons to the banks where the IRS thought the Simons were hiding money. But no, the IRS-CID Special Agent involved felt that the right thing to do was to make material misrepresentations to a magistrate judge so he would sign a **sealed** search warrant that would "legally" allow this armed commando raid on a defenseless American housewife and her youngest daughter. Denise admitted in her suicide notes "that she was terrified of the Government" and "she was not strong enough to fight." Despite protesting her and her husband's innocence, she admitted, "I just don't have any faith in the legal system, and I can't fight this." And she worried that by fighting, "I can only bring danger to my family now."

Where are the beers in the Rose Garden for Jim Simon and Special Agent Paul Muschell? Special Agent Paul Muschell works for the Secretary of the Treasury, who himself was accused of either cheating on his taxes or making some dumb mistakes for such a smart guy. Where is the Attorney General's outrage? Unfortunately for both Jim and Denise Simon, they are both white, middle class, hard working Americans, so there is no question that this terrible incident was not motivated by race or sexual orientation, which seem to be the only issues that interest the Justice Department these days – unless they involve marijuana legalization in California or illegal immigration in Arizona. Protection of the American taxpayer's Constitutional rights is not even on their radar screen.

Denise Simon is dead and she was killed by Special Agent Paul Muschell just as if he had actually pulled the trigger. The IRS Restructuring and Reform Act of 1998, and the Webster Commission Task Force of 1999 were meant to end these armed commando raids on unarmed and totally innocent American citizens. The "cowboys" out there like Special Agent Muschell and Special Agent Schrader need to be stopped and brought to justice before their lies to magistrate judges kill someone else.

But if the President will not protect you, and the Attorney General and the Department of Justice will not protect you, who can you trust to help you? Well, that brings us full circle as to why you need to vote

Republican in this upcoming election. Because the same Congressman and Senator that is **powerless** to help you regulate abortion, the death penalty, gay marriage, or guns and drugs in the streets, is exactly the person who can vote to curtail the monstrous, illegal and unconstitutional activities of the IRS. If you do nothing, the President wants to hire 16,000 more Special Agents like Muschell and Schrader to come after your family or ours. Only Congress can stop that. If you vote for the Democrat this November, you assure that starting next year you will need to report on a Form 1099 any **purchase** you make, whether it is guns, gold, or even illegal drugs. Why was that put in the Healthcare bill? Why didn't any of the Democrats read the Bill before voting on it? Why would they vote for a provision like that if it is not to curtail your freedom? You certainly cannot blame the Republicans for that Bill.

Regardless of who is to blame for the current state of affairs, your future financial security, freedom, and even your life are on the line this time. The wealthy know how to avoid taxes. The big corporations all incorporate offshore and legally pay no taxes. So why do the Special Agents of the IRS-CID pick on people like Denise and Jim Simon? *Because they can.* You do not see Special Agent Schrader planning an IRS-CID raid on Goldman Sachs, do you? Special Agent Muschell and Special Agent Schrader will not be stopped by the President, the Attorney General, or the current Department of Justice. It is only when the IRS is made to account for its actions in front of a new Republican Congress that you will be safe from unauthorized Government intrusions into your affairs and your homes due to the President's misguided intentions. This Book was written to help you and your family, and we pray that we are not too late.

TABLE OF CONTENTS

BOOK I
LEGALLY PAY NO TAXES

BOOK II

CHANGE AMERICA

BOOK III
SAVE THE WORLD

BOOK I

LEGALLY PAY NO TAXES

"The art of Government is to make two-thirds of a nation pay all it possibly can pay for the benefit of the other third."
- Voltaire

I. Killing the Death Tax

Contrary to what most wealthy people believe, the Estate Tax has always been a "voluntary" tax. It is fairly easy – and wholly legal and legitimate – to structure one's affairs to avoid the Estate Tax. For example, Warren Buffett will avoid the Estate Tax entirely by leaving his great wealth to his own private foundation and the Bill and Melinda Gates Foundation. If one wishes to leave his fortune to his heirs without paying any Gift or Estate Taxes that is a bit more problematic, but still eminently possible and legal. This is one of the primary motivations for writing this Book.

Several years ago a well-known small business lobbying firm convinced 4,000 of America's richest families to give a non-deductible $5,000 contribution to their organization to lobby for the permanent repeal of the so called "Death Tax," which will be back in full force by January of 2011. We will offer to show these same 4,000 families the simple secrets of estate planning so that they can totally avoid any Estate, Inheritance or Gift Tax, or even the Generation Skipping Tax. We will charge the same $5,000 – but make it totally tax deductible as a business expense – and then turn over all of the profits to several charitable trusts just as the late great actor Paul Newman did for the past generation through his company Newman's Own.

Of course, you could read David Cay Johnston's classic book

"Perfectly Legal" and learn the story of a famous New York City tax attorney who routinely charged his wealthy clients $250,000 for similar programs and offered a trust that was not as effective as ours, for which we charge only $5,000. Furthermore, unlike us, the Park Avenue attorneys you use would most likely not donate their fees to Charitable Trusts as we intend to do.

You could also learn these estate planning secrets from a select group of insurance agents who place business with top-rated insurance carriers. Although there are 1,800 companies licensed to sell life insurance in America, we would only recommend working with the top 25-30 carriers that are well capitalized to make sure that they will still be around many years from now when the death benefit obligation of the life insurance policy would come due. Many of the best insurance agents in the country are attorneys or CPAs by background, and you need only make three or four phone calls to your local big law firms and big regional accounting firms to find the right insurance agent for your family.

We can provide you with everything you need to work with your attorney and accountant. With our instructions, trust documents, do-it-yourself kits and checklists, you will be able to use any CPA or attorney of your choosing – and yes – you can give the insurance business to your local insurance agent. It is your money, your family, and your business. We just do not want to see you give your hard-earned

1

money to self-interested and ineffective lobbyists in the guise of civic

or business organizations for ridiculous ideas such as the repeal of the

Estate Tax, because that will never happen. And remember, no one has

advocated or even suggested the repeal of the Gift Tax. The Gift Tax

never left, and the IRS has been relentless in going after Family Lim-

ited Partnerships and Charitable Family Limited Partnerships. That

is all we are going to say about those two estate planning techniques,

however, because they are fraught with danger and we do not recom-

mend or utilize those methods.

II. Why Would Anyone Want a Defective Trust?

Art Linkletter was one of the great comedic minds of the last century, as well as an outspoken critic of both the Income Tax (way too high at marginal tax rates over 90%) and the Estate Tax (he thought it should not exist). We are reminded of his famous TV show, "Kids Say the Darndest Things" and of a particular episode where, to console a young boy who had just lost his first and only dog – a beautiful Golden Retriever that was the love of his young life – Linkletter says, "Don't cry Billy, Spot is probably up in Heaven with God right now." Billy, with all of the righteous indignation that he can muster at his young age retorts, "What would God want with a dead dog?" The same might be said in the estate planning business: "Why would anyone want a defective trust?" Or, for that matter, an "intentionally" defective trust?

Once you start down this path, you will learn that there are certain types of Irrevocable Trusts that will, in fact, allow the settlor to avoid all estate taxes. Irrevocable Life Insurance Trusts (ILITs), for example, allow large amounts of life insurance to go to the next generation Income, Estate, and Gift Tax free. But to ensure that premium contributions to an ILIT are considered gifts of a **present interest** as opposed to a gifts of a **future interest** – which are not excludible from the Gift Tax – you must use a version of a "Crummey Trust" based on the famous Californian case <u>Crummey v. Commissioner</u>, 397 F.2d 82 (9th Cir. 1968) (not to be confused with disparaging remarks about the quality of the trust). In a similar vein, when you read or hear of an "IDIOT" trust, the IDIOT acronym stands for various combinations of "<u>I</u>ntentionally <u>D</u>efective for <u>I</u>ncome taxes <u>O</u>nly <u>T</u>rust."

Since an ILIT holds tax-free life insurance policies, the Grantor (Settlor, Donor, or Creator of the trust) – or whoever established the trust – probably does not care if the trust is "defective" for income tax purposes because there will be little or no taxable income or proceeds flowing back to the Grantor. That is what "defective" for income tax purposes means. Whatever taxable income there is in the trust is taxable to the Grantor and not the trust. You will soon learn that this is a good thing, not a bad thing, especially if your goal is to avoid any Estate Taxes on the insurance proceeds and exclude any Gift Taxes on the contributions made to the trust to pay premiums.

By having the Grantor responsible for the non-existent income taxes, the trust does not need to worry about Gift Taxes because the trust and the Grantor are considered to be a single entity by the IRS – thus no "gift" is incurred from one to the other. More importantly, the millions of dollars of life insurance paid out by the trust can go to the next generation Income, Estate, and Gift Tax free, and the proceeds

4

will be protected from both personal and business creditors' claims. Later on we will also discuss "How to Skip the Generation Skipping Tax (GST)." For now, suffice it to say, there is something called an Intentionally Defective Grantor Trust that allows you to escape all Estate Taxes and exclude all Gift Taxes while providing millions of dollars for the next generation Income, Estate, and Gift Tax free – and safe from the hands of creditors – business as well as personal. Instead of calling this type of ILIT a Crummey Trust or an IDIOT Trust, we have created the name G.R.E.A.T.™ Trust, which stands for Grantor Retained Equity Access Trust™, to describe our version of the Intentionally Defective Grantor Trust. With the G.R.E.A.T.™ Trust, a wealthy family can effectively avoid all Gift and Estate taxes and send millions of dollars tax-free to the next generation.

III. Introducing the G.R.E.A.T.™ Trust

In utilizing the G.R.E.A.T.™ Trust, one can put virtually unlimited amounts of money into an Irrevocable Trust without the Grantor incurring Gift Taxes or causing the insurance proceeds to be included in the deceased's estate. The biggest problem when the Crummey Trust technique is used to transform the gift of premiums from a "gift of a future interest" (which is not excludible from the Gift Tax), into a "gift of a present interest" (which is excludible up to $13,000 per donee, or $26,000 if filing married), is one would need to find 25-30 children and grandchildren to cover the entire $640,000 contribution required to pay for $10 million of insurance on Grandpa's life. The G.R.E.A.T.™ Trust offers more flexibility wherein Grandpa, Grandma, or their companies can make virtually unlimited contributions to the Trust to pay for the life insurance premiums without regard to the Gift Tax. Gift Tax returns do not need to be filed, and there are Revenue Rulings that are directly on point which allow this technique and are binding on the Treasury.

Assume for the purposes of this discussion that your entire estate consists of one building worth $10 million. Your actual estate may be worth $100 million or even a billion dollars, but the process we are about to describe does not change. In addition to or instead of a building, your estate could be comprised of publicly-held stock, closely-held stock, or even municipal bonds; but, again, the process would remain the same. For some reason, people seem to understand the concept better if we speak in terms of a house or a building. As for the $10 million number, many members of Congress, from both sides of the aisle, have advocated raising the personal Estate Tax exemption to $3.5 million or even $5 million per person. At that level, a married couple could easily pass $10 million to the next generation using traditional estate planning tools of an ABC Trust. "A" stands for the Marital Trust; "B" stands for the Residual Trust; and "C" stands for the Credit Trust. In the case of a $5 million personal exemption, the first person to die would leave $5 million in property to the "C" Trust to use up the Gift and Estate Tax Credit afforded to each individual. The remainder of the estate would be left to the spouse under the Marital estate, which could be done as a QTIP Trust, which stands for Qualified Terminable Interest Property Trust.

Mentioning the QTIP Trust technique here is purely educational, because you certainly do not and will not need it, but many attorneys will charge you for it anyway. Just as a whole cottage industry has sprung up to market Revocable Trusts to people as a way to avoid probate (a good thing), most people feel that a Will is only for young couples with children so that they can name a Guardian of their children in the event of their untimely simultaneous death (a bad thing).

Once Congress comes to its senses and does the right thing,

only the top one percent of the population will need to worry about the Estate Tax. That is the way that it was meant to be, to recycle the wealth of J.P. Morgan, Andrew Carnegie, Andrew Mellon, the Rockefellers and their families, in that order. The Estate Tax was never meant to be an issue for the "Common Man," and believe us when we say that no family farm has ever been lost to the Estate Tax, despite all of the rhetoric you hear in Congress.

From an administrative standpoint, it makes sense to raise the individual exemption so that only truly wealthy people face an exhaustive and intrusive Estate Tax audit. The Estate Tax audit is extensive because it audits every aspect of your life, and since you are dead, you cannot defend yourself. It is overly intrusive because it goes back five years and examines every possible past transaction – business or personal – to see if there were any potential gifts.

Recent available numbers show that there were 26,000 estates audited for 2008 by the IRS. Raising the exemption would cut that number in half, if not more. The Estate Tax helps to prevent the emergence of an American Aristocracy as most family fortunes are destroyed by taxes (and bad financial management) by the third generation. However, there is clearly an American oligarchy of 4,000 to 5,000 families that control everything in America, but those families change from generation to generation just as the list of America's wealthiest people or wealthiest companies changes every year.

Remember Enron? We sure do. Enron went from nothing to the seventh most valuable company in America – and now it is gone. The collapse of Enron led to a whole series of new regulations that stifle the growth of legitimate companies, but does nothing to protect America from the real crooks on Wall Street and in the financial marketplace. But we digress. One last thing, off tangent, before we get back to the topic at hand: the Unlimited Marital Deduction is reserved for only truly "married" couples under the law. No one thinks about the Unlimited Marital Deduction unless they are barred by law – Civil Unions, if you divorce and remarry, or if you have a German or Swedish wife who does not become a citizen – none of these examples count under the Marital Deduction law. In order to escape huge estate taxes you need to leave the entire estate to the young spouse (who might be the third or fourth spouse) you married instead of your natural children (who are all older than your current spouse).

For these reasons, and a great deal more, the G.R.E.A.T.™ Trust should be utilized by everyone that has a taxable estate worth over $2 million, starting next year.

IV. Using the G.R.E.A.T.™ Trust to End the DeathTax

We will now get back to the $10 million building. As mentioned earlier, the G.R.E.A.T.™ Trust stands for Grantor Retained Equity Access Trust™, and is an Intentionally Defective Grantor Trust as described under IRC Sections 672-677. It is "defective" for income tax purposes, which means the Grantor pays taxes on any income created by the Trust, but the Trust is a very effective mechanism for avoiding all Gift and Estate Taxes. The IRS considers the Grantor and the Trust to be one and the same, and it is for that reason that when the Grantor (or Settlor or Donor) contributes the $10 million building to the G.R.E.A.T.™ Trust there is no Gift Tax, Capital Gains Tax, or Income Tax due on the transfer.

The next step involves borrowing against the property. Assume for the purposes of this discussion that the Grantor borrows $8 million from the Trust. Now, the Grantor and the Trustee can negotiate the interest rate, but if you are thinking of borrowing at low rates, think again. It is actually better for the Trust, the Trustee, and the family of the Grantor to charge above market rates, as there is no benefit for charging below market rates.

While anyone other than the Grantor can be the Trustee, there are some excellent small trust companies in Delaware and New Hampshire that can help you start your own family trust company. More established trust companies in South Dakota, Alaska, and Nevada have been fighting for this business for two decades. However, Delaware and New Hampshire have the best laws for small family fiduciary trust companies, and not only do recent IRS pronouncements make that route the best way to go, but we can provide you with all of the information you need to start your own family trust company in New Hampshire or Delaware. Again, if we assume that the Grantor borrows the $8 million at 8% interest, he must pay $640,000 in interest-only payments per year to his own trust. Yes, there is a Revenue Ruling that says the entire $640,000 is deductible, but you are missing the boat.

The tax deduction of interest for the amount borrowed from the trust is only a sideshow to the main event. In one move the Grantor has legally removed $10 million from his taxable estate and, in the next move, created a binding legal obligation of another $8 million against his estate. This allows him to pay another $640,000 a year into the trust and get those additional funds outside of his estate and into the family's hands without paying any Gift Tax on the amount contributed.

Remember the problem with the Crummey Trust? Even if Grandma and Grandpa put together their combined gift exclusions, they would still need 25-30 children and grandchildren to allow a contribution to the Crummey Trust without paying a Gift Tax. As for the $640,000 that is being contributed to the Trust, what can that be used for? Well, one way it can be used is to buy a $10 million life insurance policy on Grandpa or a $20 million Second-to-Die Survivorship life insurance policy on Grandpa and Grandma. In this way, the proceeds are payable to the Trust and, in turn, are then received Income, Estate, and Gift Tax free by the next generation from the Trust.

Even if the trust does not buy any insurance; with the interest paid on the indebtedness to the G.R.E.A.T.™ Trust the Grantor immediately reduced his taxable estate by $18 million plus $640,000 each year that he lives. Regardless of whether the assets transferred were a building, a portfolio of bonds, or closely-held stock in a business, at 7% interest the original $10 million estate would have grown to $20 million in just ten years. If Grandpa did not employ his marital deduction he would pay about $9 million in Estate Taxes on his $20 million estate, leaving $11 million to the kids and grandkids. If Grandpa passed everything to Grandma upon his death and the estate grew to $40 million ten years after that, then the estate would pay $21 million in taxes upon her death, leaving only $19 million for the children and grandchildren to complain bitterly to their elected representatives in Washington as to how unfair the "Death Tax" is and that the Estate Tax must be a Communist plot.

The legitimate Estate Tax horror stories come from closely-held family businesses where Grandpa was a great entrepreneur who built a thriving business that was worth $20 million when he died, but left all of the stock to Grandma so he did not have to pay any Estate Taxes. Grandma trusted the knucklehead sons or even worse, the avaricious no good son-in-law that married their only daughter so that he could run the business. Well, you understand the point. At Grandma's death, the IRS will put an unreasonably high value on the Company as if it were still run by Grandpa instead of the knucklehead sons or the no good son-in-law, and the Government now will want 50% of the $40 million company within 9 months of Grandma's death. This forces the closely-held company to sell off the crown jewels of the family business at fire-sale prices. Often the entire Company will be sold at a discount price to a competitor just to pay the Estate Taxes.

So, let us assume that the business is sold at the IRS valued price of $40 million. For tax purposes the Buyer will want to structure an all-asset deal so that he does not need to worry about contingent lawsuits from Grandpa's skeletons in the closet, and the Buyer will be able to write up the assets and depreciate them over time. The Federal Income Tax on the asset sale of the $40 million business is $16 million, leaving $24 million to be distributed to the family. This type of distribution probably will be taxed at 40% ordinary income rates rather than the 15% capital gain or dividend rate that disappears in 2011. If the family is taxed at ordinary rates, the $24 million is taxed at 40% and reduced by $9.6 million to $14.4 million.

The family still owes at least another $6-7 million to the IRS. If they could successfully argue capital gain treatment for the liquidation distribution, the family will only be taxed $3.6 million; leaving just a little over $20.4 million to pay the $20 million tax bill. It is easy to imagine that attorney's fees, accounting fees, investment banking fees, and not to mention city and state taxes will take their toll on the amount left to the family, making the destruction of another American family business complete.

This scenario explains why most American family fortunes are wiped out by the third generation. But, needless to say, there are several other devices (discussed later in the book) that the family could have used to save the business. Imagine the difference if the family had started using the G.R.E.A.T.™ Trust early on. The original transfer of $10 million and the borrowing back of $8 million would have taken care of $18 million of the taxable estate, plus 20 years of contributing $640,000 to the trust would further reduce the estate by another $12.8 million. And, if those amounts were used to purchase $20 million of Second-to-Die Survivorship Life Insurance on Grandpa and Grandma, that would be $50 million going to the next generation safe and secure and tax-free. The family would have plenty of time and opportunity to decide what it wanted to do, but more importantly,

Grandpa would have had the ability to leave the business to a Private Family Foundation. Forty million dollars is left to the Grandpa Foundation, $50 million is left to the family in the G.R.E.A.T.™ Trust, and no money goes to Washington to pay for the out of control deficit spending.

V. Excluding the Gift Tax

Several years ago, we were asked by one of Los Angeles' most prominent law firms to examine the Irrevocable Life Insurance Trust (ILIT) of one of their clients, a household name actor who started on Broadway but now did commercials for even more famous corporate clients. The actor's endorsement company earned about $2 million a year, or just over a million dollars a year after Federal and California taxes. Each year, the actor used his after-tax income to fund his ILIT for the benefit of his children from his first marriage. As previously mentioned, one of the reasons why someone cannot enjoy the benefit of the Unlimited Marital Deduction is that all money must go to the current wife. In Hollywood it is very common for famous actors to have three or more marriages, making estate planning not just tricky, but contentious, especially in a Community Property state like California. Eight states, mostly Western states, provide for a 50-50 split of marital assets with the current spouse, but often exclude children from earlier marriages altogether. Therefore, if someone has multiple spouses and multiple children from multiple marriages, the only way to provide for the children of earlier marriages is through life insurance paid out from an ILIT that has been funded by contributions made by the Donor. This is the problem with the typical "Crummey" ILIT.

Without having a large number of donees, the Donor will be subject to a large estate tax of 55%. In the case of the famous actor, the premiums he paid were over $500,000 annually, which required Gift Tax payments each year of about $300,000. Therefore, the famous actor was paying a nondeductible $800,000 per year from his after-tax income for $10 million of insurance coverage in the Trust. The reason for purchasing $10 million of insurance through the ILIT was so that the proceeds would go to the next generation outside of the actor's estate. What could we suggest that would be better for the Actor and his family?

First, we suggested that since the actor already had an endorsement company for his endorsement and TV ad income, he should make non-deductible contributions to a welfare benefit trust to pay for the life insurance, and name his children from his first marriage as the beneficiaries of the welfare benefit trust.

Later on, we will show that contributions to a welfare benefit plan are clearly deductible to a small business (see IRS Publication 535 on Business Expenses). That is not the point at this time, however. Just by funding the insurance for the children of his first marriage through a welfare benefit plan, the actor can contribute $800,000 to the welfare benefit trust and make sure that proceeds are received by the next generation Income, Estate, and Gift Tax free. There is also no Generation Skipping Tax in the welfare benefit world.

By contributing the money to a welfare benefit trust rather than the typical "Crummey" ILIT, the non-deductible welfare benefit trust contribution allows the actor to provide the $10 million of insurance for a cost of only $500,000 – without needing to pay the $300,000 in Gift Taxes annually. The actor realized that, had this gone on for 20 years, he would have paid $1 million in income tax each year (totaling $20 million over the same period) on top of another $300,000 in gift tax each year (totaling $6 million). His family, however, would only have received $10 million.

We suggested changing insurance carriers so that now, the same non-deductible $800,000 a year would provide a $20 million payment Income, Estate, and Gift Tax free to his children. But then the actor suggested that he should also take the tax deduction for a contribution to a welfare benefit plan, which allowed the insurance broker involved to place a $40 million policy with a $1.6 million tax-deductible premium. Now the Actor's children would receive $40 million upon his death, and the Government would not be paid any Gift or Estate Taxes and would only receive about $100,000 a year in income taxes.

A similar case was brought to us by an agent for a well-known insurance company. The broker was starting her first year in the business and had been fortunate enough to get a referral to a member of one of America's wealthiest families. This family, of course, had one of the smartest attorneys in America representing them. On the phone call with the young broker and the old attorney, the old attorney did all of the talking. The first half-hour was spent discussing how smart and experienced the old attorney was, and the second half-hour dealt with how wealthy the client and the client's family were. When we first had the chance to speak, we asked a very simple question, which was: If the client truly had "more money than God," why were we even discussing the tax deductibility of a welfare benefit plan? Why not just use the welfare benefit trust to provide a large policy payable to the next generation Income, Estate, and Gift Tax free? Since the very smart attorney was suggesting that the client pay the premiums with after-tax dollars on a personal basis (the premium plus the Gift Tax) to provide the insurance for the next generation, the attorney was having the client pay over $1.2 million in premiums and Gift Tax to provide $10 million of insurance. Since there was a family company involved, why not have the family business pay the premiums through a non-deductible welfare benefit trust? There is no limit on the amount of money that a company can contribute to a welfare benefit trust for the benefit of its key employees; the only issue is how much is deductible. The welfare benefit plan is totally selective, and the funds are secure from the hands of creditors. When the client died, the family would receive $10 million free of Income, Estate, and Gift Tax from the welfare benefit plan. The same would be true for the ILIT that the veteran attorney was recommending, but after 10 years of making premium payments, the Gift Tax of $400,000 per year would be $4 million, and after 20 years – a staggering $8 million. Within nine years the premiums plus the Gift Taxes payable are more than the death benefit.

When we suggested to the veteran attorney – who had referred us into the case – that the client use the family business to pay the insurance premiums into a non-deductible welfare benefit trust, the attorney kept asking for reasons to justify the income tax deduction for these contributions. Our approach was that the Company was so large and the family so wealthy, why worry about the tax deduction when using Company dollars rather than personal dollars to pay the premiums through a trust, because that would save millions in both income taxes (i.e., constructive dividends) and millions in Gift Taxes (premiums paid to the ILIT would require gift taxes to be paid just as in the case of the famous Actor). Because we kept demurring on the question of deductibility of contributions (of course contributions are deductible), the attorney became more and more angry with us and eventually hung up the phone in a rage.

An hour later we received a call from the young agent. The attorney had had some sort of epiphany on the Santa Monica Freeway that we were right and there was no reason to worry about the tax deductibility of premiums paid into the welfare benefit trust, because it was a total victory just in using Company funds instead of personal funds and avoiding millions of dollars in Gift Tax payments each year. Moreover, unlike the famous Actor, the wealthy client was married to the same person, so the Marital Deduction was still an option. This increased the $10 million to $20 million of Second-to-Die Survivorship Insurance on both the husband and wife of the wealthy family. The young, first-year agent, received $800,000 in commissions on the sale of the life insurance plus an apology from the old attorney. We never heard from either the young broker or the old attorney again, but after both parents died, the children had very specific instructions from their father to contact us and to follow our instructions to make sure the insurance benefit was received by them Income, Estate, and Gift Tax free.

VI. Skipping the Generation Skipping Transfer Tax

The Generation Skipping Transfer Tax (GST) is equal to the full 55% of the Estate Tax and, like the Estate Tax, it too will return in 2011. It is meant to prevent Grandparents from leaving money to their Grandchildren instead of their own children or anyone that is 37 ½ years younger than the Donor. Since Generation Skipping is often done by means of a Trust, there is a lot of talk about Generation Skipping Trusts and Dynasty Trusts. The GST issue should not be confused with the more traditional estate planning problem of the Rule Against Perpetuities, which can invalidate a trust or a transfer if it occurs more than 21 years after the last named living person in the trust dies. To solve this problem, some clever estate planning attorneys used Queen Victoria's descendants, the House of Tudor, or Queen Elizabeth I's relatives and descendants as the measuring lives. Now that states such as South Dakota and New Hampshire have done away with the Rule Against Perpetuities, it is relatively easy to establish 1,000 year-old dynasty trusts or perpetual family trusts. However, the GST created by the Tax Reform Act of 1976 is meant to eliminate the creation of aristocratic dynasties by insuring that family wealth is all confiscated by the Government by the third generation. There is no other reason for this tax.

Solutions to get around this tax invariably involve gifting the maximum amount allowable under the Unified Credit that each person has. If the Unified Credit is $1 million or $1.5 million per individual and that person gifts that money "tax-free" to an ILIT, the ILIT can then use those funds to buy insurance on the life of the Donor or the lives of the Donor and the Donor's Spouse in order to purchase Second-to-Die Survivorship Life Insurance – which only pays a benefit on the death of the survivor, i.e., the second death. The "solution" that most estate planners have for avoiding the GST is to eliminate the Unified Credit on death, because if you used up your Unified Credit making gifts during your lifetime, you have no credits to be used against the Federal Estate Tax. So for 2011 – you will start on "dollar one" at a 55% estate tax. That is why it is called the "Unified Credit" – whatever you use to avoid the Gift Tax during life, is lost to you upon death.

Thus remember our famous Actor, who was paying $300,000 a year in gift taxes because he had long since used up his Unified Credit in establishing trusts and ILITs for his children of his first marriage. Also remember that no one – and we mean no one – has suggested the repeal of the Gift Tax or the Generation Skipping Tax. And if you use up your Unified Credit, depending on your age – and your spouse's age – the most death benefit that you can pass to future generations is $10 million to $20 million. Needless to say, $10 million does not go as far as it used to and that is a small amount of death benefit to give up your entire Unified Credit for.

The only thing you need to know about the GST is that every insurance carrier has been ordered by the Government to inspect your Life Insurance Trust to see if it provides Generation Skipping Tax features. On the Form 706 (Federal Estate Tax Return), the Government will strongly suggest to your Executrix or Administrator of the Estate to submit all copies of all insurance policies on your life on the Form 712, even ones outside of the estate. The reason for this is that the Government is looking to "add back" policies that were not effectively out of your estate, invalidate imperfect gifts, charge for gifts imperfectly made, and hit any generational transfer with a flat 55% tax on top of the 55% estate tax. The problem is that you are dead and unable to defend yourself, and the great crackerjack "wealth advisors" you used to set up these ideas are long since retired. Remember, a $5 million or $10 million policy brought back into the estate – and especially one hit with a GST Tax and penalties – well; pretty soon we are talking about real money there. And, remember, you used up your Unified Credit, and like the famous Actor you have already spent a bunch of money on paying Gift Taxes to buy all of this insurance to escape the "Death Tax". Imagine if it is all blown open by the well-meaning insurance carrier that asks to see your ILIT before they even pay the death claim. Once again, the only true solution for this mess

24

is to use the G.R.E.A.T.™ Trust to get around the "Death Tax" and the non-deductible welfare benefit trust to get around the Gift and GST Transfer taxes.

The welfare benefit trust will allow any entity you establish for a business purpose to fund unlimited amounts into the welfare benefit trust – only the income tax deduction is limited. Once you forget about taking the income tax deduction, you are then entitled to use a device with no limits to put millions into the next generation or the generation after that without any Income Tax, Estate Tax, Gift Tax, or any GST taxation.

VII. Saving Your Retirement Plans from Your Least Favorite Relative

Uncle Sam – yes, your Uncle Sam – has big plans for your retirement funds. He wants everyone in America to convert to a Roth IRA now and pay 30-40% in taxes on their hard-earned retirement account and then when you die he plans on taking another 70-90% of your unspent money to help fund those unfunded deficits that you have heard so much about.

Ed Slott, a CPA from New York, does an excellent job on Public Television explaining the retirement dilemma most people face. The Government has a plan for each one of us, and if we fail to do our own planning, then the Government will take most, if not all, of our money and leave a small pittance for our families and our designated heirs. And whatever you do, pay attention to your beneficiary designations as the Supreme Court has made it clear in <u>Kennedy v. DuPont Savings and Investment Plan</u>, 129 S. Ct. 865 (2009), that if you leave your ex-spouse on as beneficiary, she may receive all of your retirement funds instead of your daughter – or as in the "Pension Pickle" case, your husband may be deprived of your retirement account because you left the funds to your brother or sister before you were married and your beneficiary designation was never changed.

But those "relative" mistakes are not what we are talking about. Your least favorite relative, Uncle Sam, is waiting patiently for you to die so that he can tax your retirement accounts with not only the income tax and the estate tax, but with things like the "success tax" and "income in respect of a decedent" and wonderful sounding names like that.

Let us assume that your retirement account has done very well and grown from $1 million to $10 million to $20 million. The better the returns, the bigger the numbers, the more staggering the results of your Uncle's calculated theft of your family's retirement proceeds. The importance of this is that any money left in your retirement accounts at death belongs to Uncle Sam, or at least the majority of it does. The better your returns, the more successful you were in your investing, the bigger the piece Uncle Sam takes. That is what the "success tax" is all about – an additional 15% on excess distributions and an excise tax on over-funded pension accounts.

But for the sake of simplicity, let us focus on the interaction between the Estate Tax and the Income Tax on the typical pension or retirement account or IRA. A $20 million estate pays an estate tax of 55% or $11 million leaving $9 million to the family. But as Mr. Slott so eloquently explains, on his way to deliver the $11 million to the IRS he was mugged and the Government took away $5.5 million (in Federal and State income taxes) leaving him $5.5 million short. Mr.

27

Slott does this wonderfully with a $10 million taxable IRA, but the bigger the numbers, the more dramatic the taking by the Government. Mr. Slott then goes back to the IRA and draws down another $5.5 million which is also mysteriously attacked by the Government who take half, leaving him about $2.75 million short. As you might expect, he goes back for the $2.75 million that he is short, but now he takes a little extra out – say $2.8 million just for shipping and handling on the eventual Government mugging – and to his surprise the Government takes half of that, leaving him short by about $1.4 million. The resulting trips back to the proverbial pension or IRA "well" will eventually drain all of the funds out of it. Just to do a quick recap – and once again this carnage is caused only by the Estate Tax and the Income Tax – nothing else is listed here:

$20,000,000 "Tax-Free" IRA

Estate Tax Draw Down:	Creates Income Tax of:	Creates Shortfall of:
$11,000,000	$5,500,000	$5,500,000
$5,500,000	$2,750,000	$2,750,000
$2,800,000	$1,400,000	$1,400,000
$1,400,000	$700,000	$700,000
$20,700,000	$10,350,000	$10,350,000

This is where the concept of "Income in Respect of a Decedent" comes in to provide a little bit of relief in reducing the total taxes paid by providing offsets for income taxes paid on estate taxable amounts and reducing estate taxes by income taxes paid. But before one rejoices at that small relief, remember there is no provision here made for state inheritance taxes or other state or city taxes, the cost of probate which could be 6% on the entire $20 million, or attorneys' fees or accounting fees or any costs for filing the various tax returns. Suffice it to say, that at $20 million and above, your retirement plan really belongs to Uncle Sam.

So what can be done about losing 80-90% of your retirement funds at between $1 million to $10 million and a virtual 100% confiscation of property at $20 million and above?

Unlike other sections of this Book, buying life insurance is not the answer. Any life insurance held in a retirement plan is certainly taxable in the estate and will also certainly lead to the "success tax" and various excise taxes for over-funding. In fact, it is illegal to own life insurance in an IRA (see IRC Section 408). Taking money out will just lead to income taxes now, and even money spent on investments like real estate will invariably end up inside the estate.

The best remedy that we have seen, and perhaps the only remedy to the problem is the S.P.I.R.I.T.™ Account. S.P.I.R.I.T.™ stands for Special Protected Individual Retirement Investment Trust™ Account.

The insurance planning techniques tried over the past decade with names such as Pension Asset Transfer and Pension Maximization were all destroyed with the publication of Rev. Proc. 2005-25, which established the valuation of insurance policies under a new PERC formula of Premiums + Earnings – Reasonable Cost for term insurance. This PERC formula effectively obliterates any insurance method such as "suppressed" cash value policies or even worse, "springing" cash value policies that were effectively outlawed by Notice 89-25.

We never liked any of these strategies, but if you are still not convinced that they are dead, please read the Tax Court decision in Matthies v. Commissioner, 134 T.C. No. 6 (2010), which unlike most Tax Court decisions dealing with employee benefit plans and life insurance, is intelligent, articulate, well thought out and well written. Very few Tax Court opinions rise to the level of Matthies, and although we do not necessarily agree with the decision in Matthies, at least it is cogent and clear.

Many Tax Court decisions are under various stages of review and appeal, and once they are reviewed by a non-biased judge with some fundamental understanding of the tax law, they will be promptly overturned just like the original decision in the Crummey case was vacated by the Court of Appeals. As discussed later in this Book, the Tax Court is just an extension of the IRS and should be disbanded. The Tax Court only proves how the Internal Revenue Code has become a trap for the unwary, and the Tax Court judges – virtually without exception – protect the Commissioner and not the Taxpayer.

But we digress again. It is only important that you realize that 90% of the money in your pension plan or IRA is destined for your least favorite relative, Uncle Sam, and the accounting will be done after you are dead and gone and cannot do anything about it.

The only remedy that makes sense, is to adopt a program like the S.P.I.R.I.T.™ Account program where you use a self-directed investment account to invest in your own company or companies rather than Bill Gates' and Warren Buffett's companies.

The S.P.I.R.I.T.™ Account program is based on another Tax Court case which the IRS not only lost, but had to pay the Taxpayer's attorneys' fees for challenging the structure of the plan at issue. Several years after that, the Department of Labor issued a favorable Advisory Opinion approving this type of investment structure for everyone. This is how S.P.I.R.I.T.™ works.

The S.P.I.R.I.T.™ Account allows an individual investor to expand the legitimate and legal investments of an ordinary IRA Account into areas normally prohibited to IRAs, such as certain types of option trading, commodities, precious metals, or even collectibles. For example, while it is clear that John Smith cannot buy gold or other commodities in the John Smith IRA account, the John Smith IRA can make an investment in Smith Financial Group, LLC (SFG). Once the money is in SFG, the Company can then invest in any legal investment strategy that it desires. Similarly an IRA cannot invest in Life Insurance contracts, but once the IRA money is invested quite legally and legitimately in the shares of the Company or SFG LLC, there is no prohibition on that money being used to fund any type of insurance program or benefit plan that is desired.

The only requirement for this program is that there be a legitimate business for the company that the IRA plans to invest in. If the LLC or Company established is not actively in a trade or business or there is no legitimate business activity or purpose, then the entire transaction will be viewed as a sham by the IRS. However, if there is a legitimate business being conducted by the Company, then there is no difference between the IRA investing in the shares of IBM, General Motors, or the SFG LLC.

Thus, whatever money we have tied up in a profit-sharing plan or a pension plan can be rolled over to a S.P.I.R.I.T.™ Account at any number of Trust Companies allowing for self-directed IRA investment accounts and you can send for the S.P.I.R.I.T.™ Account package so you can set it up yourself.

The best type of entity to establish for a S.P.I.R.I.T.™ Account investment is a "partnership" style Limited Liability Corporation (LLC) with a 1% Corporate Managing Member controlled by you and 99% owned by a family trust, a grantor trust, or a G.R.E.A.T.™ Trust. With interest rates low, perhaps even forever – like Japan – you can easily justify paying 5-6% to the IRA. Now that the money is safely invested in YOUR COMPANY, LLC, you can effectively invest it anyway you want – including stocks, bonds, artwork, commodities, gold coins, stock options – things normally prohibited in an IRA. YOUR COMPANY, LLC can also set up a non-deductible welfare benefit plan – and invest in life insurance, which is also not permitted in an IRA.

Just to be extreme, if not perversely so, let us assume that after you see Ed Slotts' insightful program on PBS and read all of his excellent books, you become convinced that Uncle Sam is out to get your hard-earned retirement dollars. You further realize that at $20 million, your least favorite relative, Uncle Sam, or the Commissioner of Internal Revenue, is likely to take everything. So you prudently set up your own S.P.I.R.I.T.™ Account and move the entire $20 million into YOUR COMPANY, LLC just like the Tax Court approved in Swanson v. Commissioner, 106 T.C. 76 (1996).

Now that the $20 million is invested in bonds, Real Estate Investment Trusts (REITs), and preferred stocks earning 8% or more a year, you take that $1.6 million and buy a $40 million Second-to-Die Survivorship Policy on you and your spouse in a non-deductible welfare benefit trust. Remember there is no limit on the contributions that you make to a welfare benefit plan – only on the deductions that YOUR COMPANY, LLC may take. Assuming that you and your spouse live another 10 years or so, let us compare the results. With the traditional IRA, your ten, twenty, or even thirty million dollars would all go to the Government, whereas the $20 million invested in your S.P.I.R.I.T.™ Account and YOUR COMPANY, LLC would pay $40 million Income, Estate, and Gift Tax free from the non-deductible welfare benefit plan, plus 99% of the $20 million would go to the family tax-free from the G.R.E.A.T.™ Trust. That is $60 million going to the family whereas under the Government plan, all $20 million would go to Uncle Sam, through his minion, the Commissioner of Internal Revenue.

Caveat Warning: You can only do the S.P.I.R.I.T.™ Account program once – so make it count. The reasons for this are very complicated, and are all explained in the S.P.I.R.I.T.™ Account package. But assume that you did have $20 million invested in a pension plan, 401(k), or an IRA. Your choices are 90% or more to Uncle Sam, or $60 million to your family and beneficiaries and nothing to Uncle Sam. Now assume you only have $10 million. The numbers are 85% to Uncle Sam, or $30 million-$50 million to your family and beneficiaries.

VIII. How to Eliminate the Capital Gains Tax and the Dividend Tax for Good

Every night, America's favorite investment guru talks about which stocks to buy or sell and offers to explain the inexplicable of why the stock market goes up or down when we least expect it. He also states at least once every show that his Charitable Remainder Trust (CRT) owns a position in one or more of the stocks that he is pounding the table for or defending. Surely he does this to pay homage to the rules of full disclosure, but surprisingly he never touts the tax advantages of his own CRT. Imagine what a service he would be doing for his viewers if he dedicated a portion of just one program a week to tout the advantages of having a CRT rather than a particular stock or investment strategy. The advantages of a CRT are as follows:

- Can eliminate capital gains taxes on the sale of appreciated assets;
- Eliminate estate taxes;
- Reduce current income taxes with an immediate charitable tax deduction;
- Substantially increase your tax-free income and investments throughout the rest of your life and avoid probate;
- Create a significant future charitable gift to the charity of your choice;

- Shelter future investment income just like a pension plan;
- Secure assets from the hands of creditors.

But what if America's favorite investment guru went on the morning talk shows and said "Don't worry about the future increase in the capital gains rate or the tax on dividends because if you use a CRT like I do, you won't pay **any** taxes." No capital gains, no tax on dividends, and no tax on ordinary income or interest from stocks or bonds. No taxes at all. Now that is a program that we would all watch.

It does not matter one bit what Congress does next year or the year after that, because you will not pay taxes on your investment portfolio – <u>ever again</u>. Imagine a trust that you control; you are the Grantor, Settlor, Donor, and Trustee and you can choose what stocks or bonds you want to invest in and when to buy or sell them. You can choose an income stream from 5% - 20% that is payable to you and/or your spouse for the rest of your life. You pay no taxes, assets are secure from the hands of creditors and there is no gift tax or estate tax to worry about. Upon your death or your spouse's death, the proceeds in the CRT go to your family foundation where, of course, your children or grandchildren are the directors.

Worried that it sounds too good to be true? Worried that the laws for CRTs are going to change? The rules for CRTs have been the same – with a few minor adjustments – since 1969. You know all those millionaires in the Senate? It is estimated that 90 out of 100 Senators have one or more CRTs in their families and about half of the Senators on both sides of the aisle have family foundations. The President and even his original Chief of Staff have CRTs and Private Foundations. The tax laws may change, but the basic tax benefits of CRTs will not.

How do you get started? We can provide you with all the forms you need from the website listed in back of this Book. We will only focus on stocks, but CRTs can, and regularly do, accept a wide variety of assets, including but not limited to cash (contributed at regular intervals) and any highly appreciated assets. Yes – it is true – when you contribute your highly appreciated stock portfolio to a CRT you do get an income tax deduction for that contribution. The tax deduction is not as big as it would be for a gift to a public charity, but that tax deduction is not what this Book or this chapter is about. Forget about it. Literally, do not take the income tax deduction for the gift made to the charitable trust.

Let us assume that you have $1 million worth of IBM or Phillip Morris stock that Grandpa said "Never sell." Your basis in the stock is only $100,000 so you are thinking that you better sell this year and make the best of a bad situation by paying 15% capital gains, because next year it might be 20% or even 40%. Instead, you can avoid any tax at all by contributing the stock to the CRT – even if you sell it inside the CRT there is no tax. You are only earning $30,000-$40,000 a year in dividends which will be next to nothing after a 40% dividend tax next year. But Grandpa said to never sell this stock. And if the turbulence of the stock market frightens you, there are a number of high dividend-paying stocks that stay relatively stable and yet pay high consistent dividends. None of these dividends will be taxable inside the CRT.

An effective investment strategy inside the CRT is to write (sell) options – both puts and calls – against Grandpa's favorite stock. This strategy can bring in 2-3% per month in steady income for the investment portfolio. At 24% per year, money doubles every three years (see, e.g., Rule of 72). So if we contribute the $1 million of Grandpa's stock – and we follow his "admonition" to never sell – we can still make $20,000-$30,000 per month in option premiums and $40,000-$60,000 per year in non-taxed dividends.

There are many companies that offer Dividend Reinvestment Programs (DRIPs) in which the quarterly dividend can be received as shares of stock and automatically reinvested into new shares of stock. Periodic dividend increases over time, and when combined with the DRIP feature and stock splits, it can create super returns in 10-20 years. This would explain why Grandpa suggested never selling that particular stock in the first place. Nothing is taxable in the CRT, as long as you stick to traditional investments such as stocks and bonds, and avoid any investments that would trigger an Unrelated Business

Income Tax (UBIT) under IRC Section 512. If you are hearing about CRTs for the first time here, and you stick to stocks and bonds or any other investment that you can make online through one of the popular trading firms, you will have no problem with UBIT taxation.

Assuming that you just used a conservative options investment strategy in a CRT, Grandpa's $1 million would grow as follows:

Year 3	$2,000,000	Year 18	$64,000,000
Year 6	$4,000,000	Year 21	$128,000,000
Year 9	$8,000,000	Year 24	$256,000,000
Year 12	$16,000,000	Year 27	$512,000,000
Year 15	$32,000,000	Year 30	$1,024,000,000

Yes – One Billion dollars in the space of one generation. Grandpa would be very proud.

Please note that in Year 30 alone, the required annual 5% distribution would be over $50 million for the year – from the billion dollar CRT investment account. This is a conservative investment strategy involving no other annual contributions other than Grandpa's favorite stock – which he said to never sell. By using a CRT you can make your Grandpa happy, never sell the stock, collect millions of dollars in dividends and stock options, make a billion dollars tax free, and contribute the billion dollars to a family foundation upon your death just as Warren Buffett or Bill Gates plan to.

If you make your children the directors of the family foundation like David Packard did, their job would be to distribute $50 million a year to charity or 5% of the principal of the foundation each year. If your children used the same investment strategy, and distributed the required 5% each year, the family foundation would grow to over $32 billion as follows:

Year 1	$1 Billion
Year 4	$2 Billion
Year 8	$4 Billion
Year 12	$8 Billion
Year 16	$16 Billion
Year 20	$32 Billion

If we have shown you how to perpetuate your family's wealth from generation to generation without paying any income, estate, or gift tax, the least you can do is name the foundation after your Grandpa.

IX. The Property Exchange

Virtually all tax attorneys and most accountants know the requirements of an IRC Section 1031 tax-free property exchange, or as it was originally called, a "Starker Exchange" based on the name of the tax case that created the technique.

The gist of the basic property exchange is that the Seller of an appreciated property can either sell the property outright and pay the capital gains tax in the year of the sale or, instead, the Seller can use the services of a Qualified Intermediary (QI) to permanently defer the taxes on the sale of the property. In the second, more efficient scenario, the Owner sells the property to the same potential buyer, but instead the proceeds from the sale are directed to and held by the QI until the Seller finds a replacement property to purchase. The Seller has six months to reinvest the proceeds in similar investment properties.

The basic Starker Property Exchange has not evolved over the years to include creative transactions such as Reverse Exchanges, Partnership Exchanges, and Exchanges that result in investments in large Tenants-in-Common (TIC) investment properties. The only thing that could possibly go wrong with this strategy would be if the QI makes a mistake in the process or if the QI absconds with the money as happened in the Virginia case of <u>United States v. Okun</u>, 2009 U.S. Dist. LEXIS 76749 (2009). The FTC has turned down many requests over the years to regulate the QI industry, despite the one or two bad apples out there. There are ways that sellers can protect themselves, however, from fraudulent and corrupt QIs by clever and conservative draftsmanship in the exchange agreements for each transaction.

There is no real reason to keep Section 1031 in the Tax Code because it is a technique that is used only by the wealthy and large corporations to circumvent the capital gains taxes, especially at times like these when the capital gains tax is scheduled to increase in 2011. The Section 1031 Property Exchange is disguised as a "tax-deferred" exchange, but it is really a tax-free exchange. Imagine a young real estate entrepreneur starts with just one rental property that costs $100,000 with a $20,000 down payment (see the HomePath program where foreclosed homes all over the country can be purchased with just 10% down). The beauty of rental properties is that the Buyer can enjoy rent that pays off the mortgage and the tax-free appreciation over time. If the young real estate investor does well and just sells his property every five years using the Section 1031 Property Exchange, he can have the following "tax-free" results:

Year 1 $20,000 Buys $100,000 Property

Year 5 $100,000 Profits Buys $500,000 Property

Year 10 $500,000 Profits Buys $2,500,000 Property

Year 15 $2,500,000 Profits Buys $10,000,000 Property

Year 20 $10,000,000 Profits Buys $50,000,000 Property

Year 25 $50,000,000 Profits Buys $250,000,000 Property

Year 30 $250,000,000 Profits Buys Out Donald Trump and starts his own television show.

There is no valid purpose or reason to keep Section 1031 in the Tax Code other than to satisfy all of the real estate moguls in the Country and increase the ever growing disparity between the rich and the poor in America.

Why Everyone Needs a
Delaware Corporation

The Joint Committee on Taxation estimates that 97% of American
business owners would **not** be affected by higher taxes brought on
by the expiration of the Bush Tax Cuts in 2011. This Book is written
for the 750,000 business owners that **everyone**, from the President, to
both sides of Congress, to the Joint Committee on Taxation, to all of
the magazines and news shows, freely admits will be expected to be
hurt by the dramatic increase in tax rates in 2011. The President has
stated that the continuation of these tax increases would result in over
$700 billion in lost revenue that the Country cannot possibly afford.
That number, of course, is dwarfed by the cost of the various stimulus
packages, the TARP Program and the cost of two wars that many probably agree should have been fought in a different way – or not at all.

The problem with most of the Government's statistics is that it
is estimated that 80% of America's 32 million businesses are sole-
proprietorships or unincorporated businesses. That means two things:
first, the 25 million businesses that are currently unincorporated are
all run by uninformed and ill-prepared people. Let us repeat that. In
this litigious world filled with increased lawsuits, IRS Criminal Investigative Division (IRS-CID) storm troopers, increased regulation, and

increased taxation, you are silly to expose yourself and your family business to unlimited liability in this society. There is **no** excuse for not being incorporated these days because a 100% owned Limited Liability Company (LLC) reports its taxes on a Schedule C of the Form 1040, just as a "sole proprietorship" does. So there is nothing complicated about accounting for your small business as an LLC as opposed to a sole proprietorship, which does nothing to protect you from our litigious society.

Second, many of the employee benefits that we will address shortly are unavailable to sole proprietorships. So to take advantage of any type of "employee benefit" plan, you must be incorporated as a C-Corp, an S-Corp, or an LLC. Virtually nothing is deductible to a sole proprietorship because the "business" and the "owner" are one and the same according to the IRS.

Most successful small businesses are already either Sub-S Corps or LLCs, which means that profits can pass through to the owners of the companies without the double taxation of a C-Corp. Even a cursory review of local business newspapers will show hundreds of LLCs being formed for each C-Corp that is created. Most of the Public companies that you can name are C-Corps, which means that they must pay taxes on their income before they distribute their profits to their shareholders in the form of taxable dividends. Dividend taxation should be eliminated, but until it is, big company shareholders will pay up to

85% of their profits in prohibitive income taxes.

In fact, the same Joint Committee on Taxation report shows that 19,000 of the 750,000 small businesses that will be affected by the increase in taxes had more than $50 million a year in revenues. All of those businesses are Sub-S Corporations and LLCs that pass through profits to the owners without any corporate taxation. Every one of those 19,000 businesses should be using the ideas described in these chapters.

For example, remember the famous Actor who was paying $300,000 in Gift Taxes just so he could contribute $500,000 in premiums to his Irrevocable Life Insurance Trust? He has several LLCs and Sub-S Corps that can make the same insurance premiums tax deductible to the Company as opposed to being after-tax personal expenses to him. Instead of paying $500,000 in premiums and $300,000 in Gift Taxes to purchase a $5 million policy, the Actor could use $800,000 after tax to buy a $10 million policy with no Gift Taxes. Once the Actor uses an employee benefit plan such as a welfare benefit trust, the Actor's LLC would be able to take a tax deduction of $1.6 million for the premium for a $20 million policy that goes to the next generation Income, Estate, and Gift Tax free – with no Generation Skipping Transfer (GST) Taxation. Remember, the Actor's company would have $2 million in endorsement income, and if he did absolutely nothing, he would either pay $800,000 in income tax, leaving $1.2 million after tax to pay $800,000 for $10 million of life insurance, or pay $800,000 in the form of $300,000 in Gift taxes and then $500,000 in life insurance premiums for only $5 million in insurance.

Thus, the true impact of the sunset of the Bush Tax Cuts will be felt by those 750,000 businesses that are making more than $250,000 but are not protecting themselves by incorporating as a C-Corp, a Sub-S Corp, or an LLC. The Government thinks that it is only raising taxes on Entertainers, Fat Cat Doctors, Wall Street Executives with rental income, and the infamous and hated Hedge Fund Managers that have dozens of LLCs streaming income up to their tax-free offshore companies. In reality, none of those people will be paying taxes because they can afford to get the best tax experts that money can buy in order to reduce their tax burden to zero, or close to it.

Therefore, the people who should take advantage of this Book – whether Republican or Democrat – are the more than 25 million small business owners that are unincorporated. Incorporate your business so that you can protect yourself and your family with limited liability protection of your home, your personal assets, and real property from lawsuits, and so you can enjoy some of the tax planning alternatives that big companies take advantage of each year to legally pay no taxes and compensate their top executives.

The best place to incorporate, based on the ease of incorporation, and for corporate governance purposes, is Delaware. No matter where they actually operate, most public companies are incorporated in Delaware. There are several large companies that can help incorporate your business in Delaware, whether you live in New York, Florida, Washington, or California.

The only drawback to incorporating in Delaware is that most states will consider Delaware to be a foreign state so that you may need to pay extra fees each year for both your home state to register as an out-of-state entity and for Delaware to have an agent for service of process. These are minor charges that you can discuss with your CPA, but the price for limited liability protection is very little and the ability to take tax deductions for items that are not deductible to a sole proprietor make incorporating in Delaware a "no-brainer" decision for the modern American business.

XI. Why Everyone Needs a Wyoming LLC

Most books on tax avoidance – which is totally legal, as opposed to tax "evasion" which is not only illegal but totally unnecessary – recommend Nevada as the best state to incorporate an LLC because Nevada does not share tax information with the Federal authorities. We do not believe that will be true much longer – if, in fact, it is true now. States like California make it known that they share and exchange information with the IRS on a regular basis. Therefore, if you lose an IRS audit in California, it is only a matter of time before you will be contacted and assessed by the California Franchise Tax Board (FTB). The encumbrances and inconveniences created by the FTB are why so many successful California businesses are incorporated in Nevada, despite having all of their operations in California.

Whatever the reason Nevada feels it needs to change its protocol for sharing information with the IRS, it appears to be happening. Wyoming, on the other hand, seems to be keeping its independent, Western-maverick spirit and is not sharing information with the Federal government. Wyoming is also the state that created and led the LLC tradition in this Country.

As previously stated, a 100% owned LLC is considered a "disregarded" entity and the 100% owner is taxed like a sole owner or sole proprietor. We would recommend that an LLC should have at least two partners so that you can use the "check-the-box" regulations to determine that your LLC is a partnership LLC up front at the time of creation. This means the LLC will not pay taxes at all, but rather will operate as a pass-through entity and all income will flow through to the partners. We recommend that one of the partners be a Delaware C-Corp that owns 1% of the LLC and acts as the Managing Member and the Tax Matters Partner (TMP) of the LLC. Your CPA will understand those terms even if you do not. The 99% partner can be a tax exempt entity such as a CRT, a Roth 401(k) or a Roth IRA – like the S.P.I.R.I.T.™ Program, or even a Domestic International Sales Corporation like the <u>Swanson</u> case. In any event, the Delaware C-Corp receives a K-1 of 1% of the pass-through entity, and the tax-advantaged or tax-exempt entity receives a K-1 of 99% of the LLC's income. Therefore, it is readily apparent that there is no reason to risk jail time by having undisclosed money in a Swiss Bank account or engaging in obvious tax shelters as were promoted by the former Big Four accounting firms.

In fact, all of those 750,000 small businesses that have more than 10 employees can change their LLC status to a C-Corp to create an Employee Stock Ownership Plan (ESOP), where the owner of the business can sell the company to the ESOP, get all of his money out tax-free, control the Company until the day he dies, and turn the Company into a tax-exempt entity by converting to a Sub-S Corp that is 100% owned by the ESOP. The Company can become 100% tax-exempt without the loss of control by the owner. The significance of this is that there is no reason to risk jail time, millions of dollars in taxes, penalties and interest, and millions of dollars in attorneys' fees as did many owners who sold their businesses and then relied on Ernst & Young or KPMG to shelter the transaction with BLIPs, OPISs, or Son of Boss tax shelters.

The Tax Code is composed of six volumes: one book of tax legislation (the "Tax Code") and five books of tax regulations, with each book longer than the King James Bible. The Tax Code's pages contain a myriad of secrets as to how to live and die tax-free in America. You just need the assistance of an experienced practitioner to help you find the right chapter and verse for your financial salvation.

XII. Why Everyone Needs a Vermont Captive

At this point, it is important to reiterate that whatever you have heard that you can do offshore to "evade" taxes, we can show you how to do the same or better onshore to legitimately avoid taxes, which is not only legal but is the cornerstone of American tax planning. As best stated by Judge Learned Hand in Helvering v. Gregory, 69 F.2d 809, 810 (2d Cir. 1934):

Anyone may arrange his affairs so that his taxes shall be as low as possible; he is not bound to choose that pattern which best pays the treasury. There is not even a patriotic duty to increase one's taxes.

And in Commissioner v. Newman, 159 F.2d 848, 850-51 (1947), he wrote:

Over and over again, courts have said that there is nothing sinister in arranging one's affairs as to keep taxes as low as possible. Everybody does so, rich and poor; and all do right, for nobody owes any public duty to pay more than the law demands: taxes are enforced exactions not voluntary contributions.

Captive insurance companies were once hated by the IRS, but recently all of the IRS's rulings and regulations have been pro-captive and make owning or participating in a captive insurance company one of the most exciting tax-saving opportunities for any American business.

The only tax-saving strategy that was on the original Listed Transaction List of IRS Notice 2002-70 that was subsequently taken off the list was the description of how an American company could establish a Producer Owned Reinsurance Company (PORC) in, say, Barbados or Bermuda or some other offshore haven for captives. The company could then claim to be taxed as a small American insurance company, pay little or no taxes inside the captive, and have millions of dollars accumulate tax free. As discussed elsewhere, the captive insurance company is a tax loophole technique used by virtually every large company in America that allows them to save billions of dollars each year. That is why it is a mystery that the IRS has effectively outlawed IRC Section 419A(f)(6) plans by instituting large fines under Section 6707A against participating employers, but at the same time has taken the captive insurance company off the "listed transaction" list. See IRS Notice 2002-70 and IRS Notice 2004-65.

The significance of this is that the IRS has effectively eliminated multiple employer welfare benefit plans under IRC Section 419A(f)(6) by imposing egregious penalties that even the National Taxpayer Advocate Nina Olsen refers to in her annual report as "unconscionable" and "unconstitutional":

> *Section 6707A of the Code imposes a penalty of $100,000 per individual per year and $200,000 per entity per year for failure to make special disclosures of a "listed transaction." Enacted in 2004 to help combat tax shelters, this penalty is having unconscionable and possibly unconstitutional impact on taxpayers who have done nothing wrong.*

National Taxpayer Advocate - 2008 Annual Report to Congress, pg. 13. (Emphasis added).

The IRS has eviscerated and effectively destroyed the IRC Section 419A(f)(6) business by imposing these Draconian penalties and investigating plan administrators with a needless, feverish enthusiasm, causing them to incur hundreds of thousands, if not millions, of dollars in accounting, legal, and consultancy fees just to defend themselves against the IRS's audit grist mill. The absurd comedy, or tragedy, of the government's endeavor is that in its most fertile season, the 419A(f)(6) industry had a total market volume of $100-150 million, which is less than Exxon's 2009 tax refund of $150 million, but no one is going after Exxon with illegal IRS-CID raids and Section 6707A penalties. At the same time the IRS is marauding the welfare benefit plan landscape, looking to destroy small businesses through audits and egregious penalties; it issues Revenue Rulings and Regulations that allow the captive business in the United States alone to exceed $500 billion a year. That is a lot of tax deductions for a lot of businesses that effectively are contributed to a tax-exempt captive, never to be taxed again.

Once the money is in the particular captive, there is no limit on loaning money back to the parent at favorable interest rates which are being kept artificially low by the Government. The rates are being kept so low, that big companies like Microsoft say that it is better for them to keep loaning money from their offshore companies (or borrowing domestically at unprecedented low rates) rather than repatriating the money back to the United States.

Imagine your local car dealer or the owner of your local burger joint. Both of these "small" businesses have the potential to make a million dollars a year, and they are clearly in that group of the 750,000 business owners that will be affected by the sunset of the Bush Tax Cuts. Most local car dealers have several franchises at different locations, and most fast food entrepreneurs own 10-20 different restaurants with 100-500 employees. Imagine the possibility of legitimately taking your entire bottom-line net-operating income and putting it into an entity that you control and that effectively pays no taxes. This is what makes the captive insurance company such an exciting idea. And whereas the IRS has all but outlawed Section 419A(f)(6) plans and put them all out of business, the IRS has made captive insurance companies not only feasible, but now almost a mandatory part of any successful entrepreneur's tax planning. Remember, captives afford a full tax deduction for contributions going in, the funds accumulate tax free, the funds can be returned at capital-gain rates or even tax free, and the funds are always there when you need them to pay for insurance claims or other business expenses.

This is where Vermont comes in. Whereas most of the United States had no captive insurance industry, Vermont under Governor Howard Dean established a robust onshore captive industry to compete with and rival Bermuda, Barbados, and even the Turks & Caicos, which ruled the PORC and credit life captive insurance markets. Now in the top 10 listings of domiciles for captive insurance companies worldwide, Vermont has recently issued its 900th captive insurance license and now ranks third behind only Bermuda, the longtime traditional captive favorite, and the Cayman Islands as a domicile for creating a captive insurance company. Where Vermont is proud that they have 40% of the Fortune 500 as satisfied parents of Vermont captives, the more impressive number is $140 billion in assets under management. This has all happened in the space of ten years, since captives, unlike 419A(f)(6) plans, were taken off the Treasury's hit list of "listed" transactions. So-called 419 plans – meaning 10-or-more employer plans as described under IRC Section 419A(f)(6) – have been hunted down by a zealous IRS that wanted to administer out of existence a Congressionally mandated welfare benefit trust that was meant to be the complement and reciprocal of a Union's collectively bargained IRC Section 419A(f)(**5**) **multi-employer** benefit plan. Union plans are alive and well under Section 419A(f)(5), whereas private company plans for trade associations and non-union plans are all but extinct under Section 419A(f)(6). But during the same time frame of just 10 years captives have undergone the opposite change. IRS Notices 2000-12 and 2000-15 – establishing the so-called "listed transactions" list – were issued on February 29, 2000. Captive insurers did not come off the list until 2004 with the issuance of IRS Notice 2004-65. And, in about six years, Vermont has gone from the number 20 domicile in the world to a dominant number 3 with hundreds of billions of tax-deductible dollars coming in the next decade.

There is so much information just on the Vermont captive website on the advantages of creating a captive insurance company that there is no reason to replicate that information here. Suffice it to say, that it is certainly quite possible for all of those companies in the "unlucky" 750,000 whose taxes will dramatically increase at the expiration of the Bush Tax Cuts to do their own tax planning, participate in a captive insurance company somewhere, legally pay no taxes, control the company, and get all of the money back some day tax-free, just as Microsoft, IBM, and Exxon have all done just in this past year. One could never do that with an ordinary multiple-employer 419 welfare benefit plan. Now it is too late to stop the growth of captives, which, in Vermont alone, every year dwarfs the income of most small nations.

XII. Why Everyone Should Have a New Hampshire Trust Company

Like its neighbor Vermont has done in captive insurance companies, New Hampshire plans to dominate the private family trust company business through the passage of several favorable laws. Prior to New Hampshire's entry, the leading states for establishing a private trust company were South Dakota and Alaska. New Hampshire has since leapfrogged all of its competitors and become the preferred state in which to incorporate a private family trust company. Once again, this is significant because wealthy families can take advantage of very favorable recent rulings from the Treasury in regard to private family trust companies and the control of life insurance trusts.

Despite the recent emergence of Nevada as a real contender in the family trust company arena, New Hampshire is still number one, closely followed by Delaware. There is a very well known tax attorney representing the various states as they compete to be number one in the private family trust company business, but he only works with families having a billion dollars or more to invest. That certainly leaves a lot of clients for the rest of us.

Imagine the ability to have your own family fiduciary trust company control the investment of insurance policies in your own

G.R.E.A.T.™ Trust. Now there is no need to leave the family fortune in the hands of corrupt Wall Street money managers or the investment dunces of the local bank trust department. Do not even think about it. Every estate planning attorney can relate horror stories of how the local bank trust company totally fouled up an estate with the wrong investments at the wrong time. For example, one family alone lost nearly $800 million in so-called safe and liquid auction rate municipal bonds.

There are so many advantages to having a family trust company that it just does not make sense not to have one. Delaware requires $1 million in assets but New Hampshire only requires $500,000 to have a private trust company. For all of the tax advantages and control advantages it offers, the family trust company is just one more "no-brainer" for successful entrepreneurs and their families.

XIV. How Many Jobs Were Created by the American Jobs Creation Act of 2004?

How many jobs were created by the American Jobs Creation Act (AJCA) of October 22, 2004? Zero. Not a single one. The same can be said – and will be said eventually – about the Small Business Jobs Act of 2010 (H.R. 5297) signed September 27, 2010.

Instead of creating jobs, an incredible web of nasty booby-traps were put into the Tax Code not just for the unwary, as is normally the case, but also for the experienced practitioner. Nina Olsen, the National Taxpayer Advocate in her 2008 Report to Congress referred to these new penalties as not just "unconscionable", but "unconstitutional" as well.

Section 6707A of the Code imposes a penalty of $100,000 per individual per year and $200,000 per entity per year for failure to make special disclosures of a "listed transaction." Enacted in 2004 to help combat tax shelters, this penalty is having unconscionable and possibly unconstitutional impact on taxpayers who have done nothing wrong. The penalty must be imposed where a taxpayer fails to make the special disclosures – even if the taxpayer had no knowledge that the transaction was listed or even questionable, even if the tax-

payer derived no tax savings from the transaction, and even
if the transaction is not "listed" until years after the taxpayer
entered into it and filed a return on which the transaction was
reflected. A taxpayer who does business through a wholly
owned S corporation is subject to a penalty of $300,000
($200,000 at the entity level and $100,000 at the individual
level) for each year in which the transaction is reflected on a
return. The requirement that this penalty be imposed with-
out regard to culpability may have the effect of bankrupting
middle class families who had no intention of entering into
a tax shelter. The National Taxpayer Advocate recommends
that Congress quickly amend § 6707A so that the amount of
the penalty bears a proportional relationship to the amount of
any tax savings realized.

National Taxpayer Advocate - 2008 Annual Report to Congress, pg. 13.

These new traps include Section 6707A, which impose a severe penalty for failing to disclose your participation in a "reportable" or "listed" transaction (all "listed" transactions are now also considered "reportable" transactions) even though most taxpayers are unsure of what either a listed or reportable transaction is, or how they may have triggered the penalty. This penalty can be imposed by an IRS Agent on an *ex post facto* basis, for hundreds of thousands of dollars (we have small business clients facing $800,000 in penalties for simply putting life insurance in a pension plan under IRC Section 412(i); those penalties are clear violations of the "excessive fines" clause of the Eighth Amendment), and worst of all, there is no judicial review of these fines by any Court. This is all in your USA Tax Code, put there by your Congressman who did not bother to read any of the 400 pages of the AJCA before he voted on it. You should send a letter to Senators Max Baucus and Charles Grassley of the Senate Finance Committee. Better yet, send them a copy of this Book.

As if Section 6707A penalties were not bad enough, recently, a husband and wife were assessed with penalties for making two annual contributions of insurance premiums from their S-Corp to a Section 412(i) pension. The penalty for their participation was $200,000 for the Sub-S Corp and $100,000 for each of them – thus $400,000 for each year and $800,000 in total. The husband and wife were assessed these inordinate penalties in 2009 because the Plan was deemed to be a "listed" transaction in 2008, even though the tax years in question were 2004 and 2005. Yes, you have got that right – the AJCA applies to all years ending after October 22, 2004, which included tax years that began **before** the Act was passed into legislation – and the Commissioner of the IRS believed that all American taxpayers read the small print of a 400-page tax bill that their Congressmen totally ignored, and that they could read the Commissioner's mind and somehow, with the gift of prophecy, foretell that the Commissioner would effectively make "illegal" in 2009 a type of retirement plan that a small business person would use in 2004 and 2005. Never mind that these Draconian penalties and procedures were not mentioned on the IRS's own website until 2007, the American taxpayer was expected to have known about these penalties in 2004 even though the law was not even created or passed until October 22, 2004, and the AJCA stated that the Act would apply to tax years ending after that date. Merely forgetting to mention in your 2004 tax return that you participated in a transaction that was "substantially similar" to one of three dozen transactions on a list that the Commissioner believes is a "potentially abusive" tax shelter could result in hundreds of thousands of dollars in penalties. You never saw any list; you never had any warning; and you certainly do not agree that your retirement plan or your benefit plan is tantamount or "substantially similar" to an abusive tax shelter.

Just to make sure the penalties were steep enough, if you engaged in one of these so-called "listed transactions," you could be hit not just with taxes and interest, but also with new penalties under Section 6662A of up to 40% for failing to provide that disclosure form – Form 8886 – that no one knows about. Go ahead – ask your Congressman when he knocks on your door asking for your vote if **he** knows what

Form 8886 is – and if he doesn't, ask why he voted for it in the AJCA of 2004. Senators Grassley and Baucus know what it is because they have sent letters to the Commissioner urging him to suspend the collection of these egregious and unconstitutional civil penalties. But this is just another example of what can happen to innocent and unsuspecting taxpayers four or five years after a transaction was completed. Section 6662A imposes a penalty equal to 40% of the value of the transaction for failing to disclose participation in a "listed transaction", but this section should not be confused with Section 6662(a), which imposes a penalty equal to 20% of the value of the transaction for negligence, which has all sorts of exceptions for "reasonable cause" or "good faith" or even "substantial authority." None of exceptions to Section 6662(a) apply to Section 6662A – not even "reasonable cause" because if you did not file Form 8886, which you did not even suspect you had a reason to file, you are not allowed to argue "reasonable cause" even if you had a dozen legal opinions saying yours was not a "listed transaction" and you had no reason to file the Form 8886.

Remember, this is only a small business problem. A big company, facing a "reportable transaction" violation would pay only $50,000 in fines, rather than the unconscionable $200,000-plus for a small business "listed transaction." But, we have not even begun to describe the most Kafkaesque of the provisions of the AJCA: the Section 6708 penalty for failing to keep or turn over a list of your clients to suffer the agonies of the IRS audit gristmill. Though this is clearly an end-run around the Congressionally mandated taxpayer protections of Section 7609(f) – the John Doe Summons Procedure – the IRS is designating certain professionals, i.e., lawyers and accountants, as Material Advisors to a transaction in order to force them to give up the names of their clients or suffer crippling fines for failing to do so.

If the IRS wants the names of unknown taxpayers from an "advisor," it must use the John Doe Summons Procedure as proscribed by Section 7609(f).

> **If the sole purpose of the summons was to find other taxpayers for the IRS gristmill the information sought from AmerUs would not be relevant to [IRS Agent] Higgins' investigation which concerns only the conduct of xélan in marketing the 419 Program and its compliance with various statutory requirements. In such a case, the identity of other participants could be obtained from AmerUs by administrative summons, if at all, only through a "John Doe" summons under the procedure outlined in IRC §7609(f).** The "John Doe" summons process requires, among other things, a court proceeding at which the IRS must establish a reasonable basis for believing that a group or class of unidentified persons may fail, or may have failed, to comply with

the internal revenue laws. Because unidentified persons have no opportunity to institute proceedings to quash such a summons, §7609(f) substitutes the Court to "take" the place of the affected taxpayer" in order to "exert" a restraining influence on the IRS" through the required findings.

xélan, Inc. v. United States of America, No. M-04-83, Order filed Feb. 7, 2005 (S.D. Iowa). (Emphasis added)

The IRS will also try to circumvent the Taxpayer protections provided by the IRS Restructuring and Reform Act (RRA) of 1998, which added Section 7491 – that shifts the burden of proof from the Taxpayer to the Commissioner once the Taxpayer submits any credible evidence – and the John Doe Summons Procedure of Section 7609(f) that requires the Commissioner to go to the US Department of Justice to get a sign-off to bring the case to a Federal Court to get a Judge to hear why the privacy of unknown taxpayers should be invaded.

As an alternative to the Congressionally required John Doe Summons Procedure, the IRS will send Third-Party Summonses to banks, insurance companies, your neighbors, and even insurance brokers to get them to reveal who their insurance clients are in the guise of a Section 6700 investigation. But, the IRS's own Summons Enforcement

Manual says that the IRS must have evidence of **all** of the following factors before launching a Section 6700 investigation:

1. There must be a "**promoter**."
2. Who in the **marketing** of
3. An "**abusive**" tax shelter
4. Has made a **false or fraudulent** statement
5. As to a **material fact**
6. Of the **nature of the tax benefits** of the program
7. That is **known by the promoter to be false.**

So the target of a Section 6700 investigation is now told that he must reveal the names of all of his clients – yes, even the ones not involved in tax shelters, and, yes, even ordinary insurance clients – or risk huge fines. But what is the penalty for the person who might actually be involved in a Section 6700 activity? How about a maximum of $1,000 – or 50% of the income received from the activity. So if you are the typical insurance broker – who is absolutely not involved in the marketing or promotion of any abusive tax shelters and you certainly did not make any false statements to anyone about anything – you say "let me pay the fine and go on my way, because if I give you the names of all of my insurance clients, and you audit them as I know you will, I will be out of business in a year." Who would want to work with an insurance agent that would end up getting them audited?

Naturally the insurance broker's attorneys all advised him to pay 15% of his fine under Section 6700, which he is allowed to do under Section 6703(c) so that he can take the issue to Federal Court. Remember, the insurance broker's actual penalty would be zero because he is not involved in any tax shelter activity, but his attorneys recommend that he pay 15% of the maximum fine of $1,000 rather than cripple his career as an insurance broker.

Strangely enough, the IRS does not accept the payment clearly provided for under Section 6703(c) because it has not been assessed yet. In reality, the IRS just wants to continue their "investigation" rather than accept the small penalty for the alleged violation. They then bring the case to Federal Court to enforce their summons asking the insurance agent to disclose all of the names of all of his clients. So, was the IRS truly interested in the $1,000 fine under Section 6700, or were they more interested in securing more names for the IRS audit mill and auditing all of the insurance broker's clients to find more people who had put life insurance in their pension plan under Section 412(i) (which everyone will tell you is perfectly legal to do)? There are thousands of taxpayers out there facing penalties of $200,000 to $800,000 on an *ex post facto* basis in clear violation of the due process clause of the Fifth Amendment and the excessive fines clause of the Eighth Amendment.

The last story of the horrors created by the AJCA – and we are not even discussing the nightmare of Section 409A because it mainly affects big companies – deals with "Material Advisor" status and who must maintain a list of their clients who were put into abusive tax shelters. To be a "Material Advisor," you must do the following:

1. You must provide material aid, assistance, or advice with respect to organizing, managing, promoting, selling, implementing, insuring, or carrying out any reportable transaction;

2. You must directly or indirectly derive gross income in excess of the threshold amount ($50,000 for reportable transactions, $250,000 in any other case) for such aid, assistance, or advice;

3. You must represent or provide education regarding listed or reportable transactions;

4. You must be paid by someone that is in the tax statement or tax advice business;

5. You must receive a commission for making
   a tax statement;

6. You must be directly related to a welfare benefit trust, and
   compensated from such trust; and

7. The insurance carrier you are licensed with that provides
   the benefit applied for by the insured has provided tax
   advice in the matter.

Clearly this is meant to be a trap for attorneys and CPAs who routinely give tax advice to clients on all sorts of matters. That is why you will see Circular 230 Notices on every email you get these days from your CPA's office or from your attorney's office even though you are using him to sue somebody or to complete a real estate transaction. The fear of being linked to "tax advice" for a "tax shelter" runs very deep at all law firms and accounting firms, as many law firms were put out of business for being "Material Advisors" to an abusive tax shelter. Even Arthur Andersen was put out of business because one accountant in one office helped Enron do some things that maybe they should not have done. In any event, most Americans do not know that Arthur Andersen was vindicated and exonerated by a 9-0 unanimous Supreme Court decision that came too late because the company had already

folded and 40,000 innocent people lost their jobs, careers and liveli-
hoods due to overzealous prosecutors. Even fewer Americans know
that certain partners at KPMG are fighting for their lives – against all
odds and with the Government's prohibition on KPMG paying their
attorney fees – because they were involved in designing tax-sheltered
transactions for their biggest and best clients. In the old days, saving
taxes for corporate clients was the highest echelon of a big law firm or
accounting firm. Now, it can end up costing you jail time.

But what if you were not a law firm or an accounting firm? What
if you never gave tax advice to anyone? And what if you never made
a dime for giving tax advice, much less the $250,000 threshold? There
is no way that you could be hit with the Section 6708 penalty for being
a "Material Advisor," right?

Guess again. Section 6708 was changed by the AJCA from a
maximum penalty of $50,000 to penalties of $10,000 a day for each
day the list was not turned over. So, imagine that you were the third-
party administrator (TPA) of a large welfare benefit plan from 1998-
2000. You ceased having anything to do with that welfare benefit plan
in 2001. In 2008, an IRS Agent makes the unilateral decision that the
welfare benefit plan was "substantially similar" to a transaction on the
listed transaction list. Now remember that Section 6708 was changed
in October 2004 for the years following 2004 to penalize "Material
Advisors" (as defined under Section 6111(b)(1)) for advising their

clients in transactions as described under Section 6111.

Obviously you are thinking that a TPA of a welfare benefit plan cannot possibly be a "Material Advisor" as defined by Section 6111(b) (1) as they make no money and they give no tax advice or tax opinions to anyone. Also you are thinking that a welfare benefit plan cannot possibly be "substantially similar" to an abusive tax shelter under any possible definition of the word. So, if you do not have a "listed transaction" or an abusive tax shelter, you cannot possibly have a list requirement under Section 6112, and therefore it would be impossible to violate Section 6708. You would be correct on all of these assumptions unless, of course, you were dealing with the IRS.

Believe it or not, a solitary IRS Agent has the ability to suspend all Constitutional rights of the taxpayer, and in 2009 an IRS Agent assessed the TPA over $1.2 million in penalties for failing to provide a list of participating employers in 2002 that was not even demanded until 2008. The TPA immediately sent letters to IRS Appeals, the National Taxpayer Advocate's office, and anyone who would listen. There was no legal requirement in 2002 to keep any list because the law was not created until October 22, 2004, and the Plan at issue was not even considered to be "substantially similar" to a listed transaction until 2008. Since the TPA had effectively stopped working with the Plan in 2000 or 2001, how could it be liable for a penalty in 2009 when there was no "list" requirement in 2002? The IRS does not need to listen to logic though, because it is the IRS and it can do anything it wants, and it is presumed correct on everything it does; see the multiple cases cited in this Book. Anyway, while the TPA was dutifully working with the National Taxpayer Advocate's office and IRS Appeals, the IRS Agent sent a Notice of Intent to Levy. This Notice gives the taxpayer 30 days to file for a Collection Due Process (CDP) Hearing, which the TPA firm did, within 10 days of receiving the Intent to Levy. The IRS, however, did not wait 30 days, and within two weeks of the Intent to Levy, they put a lien on all of the TPA's assets. Clearly this lien violates all notions of fairness and due process and is being challenged in court for violating the Constitution, and the IRS is fighting every step of the way without acknowledging the insanity of assessing a penalty in 2009 for a list that the TPA had no duty to provide in 2002. Needless to say, the assessed penalty, if it were legitimate and collectible, would put the TPA out of business. Just having the lien filed effectively destroys the TPA's financial health, which is imperative for banking purposes and state filings.

Assessing this type of excessive penalty on an *ex post facto* basis without the benefit of due process is clearly unconstitutional on a number of levels, but the President's Healthcare Bill would add 16,000 new IRS-CID agents who could come knocking on your door to check on how much gold you have in your possession. Both of those provisions – which have nothing to do with healthcare – are in the

Healthcare Bill that no Congressman read. Anyone who voted for that Healthcare Bill must be voted out of office. Another reason why every Democrat should be voted out of office is the recently signed Small Business Jobs and Credit Act of 2010 (H.R. 5297), which kept the Section 6707A penalty the same $200,000 per company, and $100,000 per individual for anyone "unknowingly" participating in any "listed" transaction:

> *(a) In General- Subsection (b) of section 6707A of the Internal Revenue Code of 1986 is amended to read as follows:*

> *(2) MAXIMUM PENALTY- The amount of the penalty under subsection (a) with respect to any reportable transaction shall not exceed--(A) in the case of a listed transaction, $200,000 ($100,000 in the case of a natural person)...*

This means that even after more than a year under Congressional review, the penalty remained unchanged so that you and your company could still be penalized a **minimum** of $300,000, regardless if you contributed $500,000 or $5 million, for participating in a transaction that the IRS identifies as a "listed" transaction three to five years after the fact, even if it turns out the transaction is perfectly legitimate and totally tax deductible.

These are the same penalties that the National Taxpayer Advocate referred to as "unconscionable" and "unconstitutional" in her 2008 report. Congress had a chance to get rid of these spectacularly absurd penalties, and yet it did not even take out the portion of Section 6707A that states that the penalties – once assessed – cannot be reviewed by a Federal Court. This type of law has been unconstitutional since Marbury v. Madison, 5 U.S. 137 (1803), created judicial oversight of the Executive Branch and the checks and balances that we count on in America. This is yet another reason to vote out every Democratic Senator and Congressman.

XV. The Tax-Exempt Oil and Gas Business

Numerous commentators and tax experts have stated that the American Tax Code gives you one of two options. You may either pay your taxes year after year as most of us do, or you can invest in tax-sheltered oil and gas deals and legitimately pay no taxes because of all of the favorable tax treatment given to oil and gas companies. It is possible for anyone to invest as little as $25,000 to create $16,000-$20,000 in current tax deductions this year for intangible drilling costs even though the drilling will not even begin until next year. And if you borrowed the $25,000 at 4% based on a home equity loan, you could establish your own private tax shelter. Strangely enough, that would not be a "listed" or even a "reportable" transaction as far as "tax shelters" go. The deductions for intangible drilling costs are considered not to be "passive" so they can be used to offset regular, ordinary income, or any type of gains.

There are so many "legitimate" tax advantages in the Tax Code for "small" oil and gas companies, it should come as no surprise that Exxon-Mobil reported $50 billion in profits (not revenues – but profits) with no taxes payable in the United States. Exxon actually received a tax refund of $150 million for its fiscal year ending 2009. Remember that for Book Three, "Save the World." Now, of course, Exxon is famous for having several offshore captives and over two dozen offshore foreign subsidiaries – some of which pay taxes and some of which pay no taxes for anything. But Exxon has not taken advantage of a tax technique called "Inversion" whereby several Houston-based oil industry businesses have reincorporated in the Cayman Islands, Bermuda, and Switzerland so that they can save billions a year in Federal taxes. Interestingly enough, three of the most famous oil companies to do this "Inversion Transaction" were all Delaware Corporations based in Houston – now made famous by the BP Gulf oil spill – including Transocean, Noble Drilling, and Nabors Industries. Not happy with all of the tax benefits already provided to the oil and gas industry in the Tax Code, these three companies reincorporated in the Caymans, Switzerland, and Bermuda respectively, but still run their businesses out of Houston and still do a lot of work in Texas and the Gulf of Mexico. The simple reincorporation in a tax exempt island country, however, allows these three companies to legally avoid paying hundreds of millions, and even billions of dollars a year in taxes in the United States.

The same famous American Jobs Creation Act (AJCA) of October 22, 2004 that created no jobs did try to take the tax benefits away from the "Inversion Transaction" by adding Section 7874 to the Code, which would effectively try to negate the tax benefits of "Inversion" done after March 4, 2003.

The actual effective date of Section 7874 is not as important as the lobbying that went into the effective date. In January 2007, the Senate

Finance Committee was looking for revenue enhancements to offset the cost of a new package of small business incentives. Additionally, several members of Congress wanted to punish Nabors Industries specifically because it sought an extension of its special exception to the Jones Act (which also became famous during the BP Gulf Oil spill Disaster) that permits **only** United States companies to ship goods between United States ports and the offshore oil rigs. The Finance Committee had debated the anti-inversion provisions of Section 7874 as early as 2001 and 2002. The Joint Committee on Taxation estimated that the backdating of the effective date would raise approximately a billion dollars from Nabors alone.

But, according to a detailed and comprehensive report in the New York Times ("The Congressman, the Donor, and the Tax Break," New York Times, Nov. 24, 2008), before the vote came up for changing the effective date, Nabors CEO Eugene Isenberg met with Congressman Charles Rangel – the powerful Chairman of the House Ways and Means Committee – who eventually opposed the Senate provision for changing the effective date of the "Inversion" transaction taxation by stating his disdain for "retroactive" tax hikes. The glib hypocrisy of Chairman Rangel's position regarding the AJCA, however, is revealed by his indifference to the myriad number of retroactive taxes and penalties contained in the AJCA and the Small Business Jobs Act of 2010, designed to cripple small businesses with huge penalties being assessed retroactively years **after** the fact for hopelessly ambiguous "listed" transactions – that are often determined to be "listed transactions" years after the small business has participated in the endeavor. These penalties can bankrupt both the company and the individual. Remember, the original list of "listed" transactions that came out on February 29, 2000 required contributions of $2-5 million to create annual tax savings of a million dollars or more.

Though both deny any *"quid pro quo,"* it is clear from the New York Times story that Isenberg of Nabors Industries pledged $1 million for the Charles B. Rangel Center at City College of New York at the same time that Chairman Rangel opposed the backdating of the effective date that almost everyone else favored. As the Times reported: "What is clear is that Mr. Rangel played a pivotal role in preserving the tax shelter for Nabors and the other companies in 2007" (Id. New York Times, Nov. 24, 2008. See also "Oil Drillers Gain Billions from Immoral Tax Break" by Martin A. Sullivan at Tax.com. Taxanalysts, June 11, 2010).

Debate over anti-inversion provisions continues to the present day in the International Tax Competitiveness Act of 2010. There are several other bills intending to limit the tax advantages the oil and gas industry enjoy, tax advantages that are in addition to the "anti-inversion" provisions, that Congress and the President both support, and that would raise billions for the Treasury. The best list of tax advantages enjoyed by the oil and gas industry can be found at Congressman Earl Blumenauer's website. Congressman Blumenauer (D-Oregon) has presented a comprehensive bill to reduce subsidies to the oil and gas industry that would raise $30 billion for the Treasury over the next five years. Senator Robert Menendez (D-New Jersey) has introduced similar legislation in the Senate. Although the purpose of this Book is to elect Republicans to the House and Senate in November 2010, credit should be given to those brave souls that would fight the oil and gas industry. All of the tax benefits of drilling should be ended. It is an anachronism that we can no longer afford.

Exxon makes an easy target for what has gone wrong with the Tax Code. Exxon has helped itself to each and every one of the tax benefits provided in the Tax Code to make it one of the largest companies in the World – if not the largest – and has done nothing wrong, immoral, or illegal. Exxon is also big enough to protect itself from IRS-CID storm-trooper raids that are being used against small businesses like restaurants, pension administrators, and innocent people like you. Those 750,000 small businesses are the ones susceptible to the imminent tax increase, the Draconian, "unconscionable and unconstitutional" penalties of the AJCA, and now the Small Business Act of 2010 for "listed" transactions, as well as raids from the new IRS-CID "wealth-squads" looking for tax violations by wealthy small business owners, even though these commando raids by the IRS clearly violate the Fourth and Fifth Amendments of the Constitution. To solve their financial crisis, they are already forming special squads of government police in Greece to invade the homes and businesses of the wealthy, and the President wants 16,000 more Special Agents to join the IRS-CID attack teams in order to descend on innocent American homes and businesses with no notice, no due process, and with sealed warrants.

"...*Every unjustifiable intrusion by the Government upon the privacy of the individual, whatever the means employed, must be deemed a violation of the <u>Fourth Amendment</u>. And the use, as evidence in a criminal proceeding, of facts ascertained by such intrusion must be deemed a violation of the Fifth.*"

<u>Olmstead v. United States</u>, 277 U.S. 438, 479 (1928)

Everyone must vote Republican in the election of November 2010 to preserve American freedoms as we know them. It is in everyone's best financial interests to return the Country back to the gridlock of 1994 and the financial gains made by everyone from 1994-2000. It is just as important to protect our civil rights and personal liberty from those who would take them away in the name of raising revenues for an ever-growing government, or for the so-called protection of society or our American way of life, whatever that may be.

XVI. How Employers Can Benefit From Employee Benefit Plans

There are several ways that employers – specifically small business employers – can take advantage of traditional employee benefit plans and take a deduction for personal business expenses. Small businesses incorporated as C-Corps can take deductions for the owner-employees as if they were just like any other employee. Small businesses incorporated as a Sub-S Corps can have the stock split between family members in such a way that if the husband or wife owns 98% or more of the company, then insurance and benefit plans can be established in the minority-owner spouse's name because the spouse owns 2% or **less** of the company. Small businesses organized as LLCs should always have two or more partners in order to avoid becoming a disregarded entity. A partnership LLC files a Form 1065 for the entity – which pays no taxes – and can treat its individual partners as employees even if they are owners.

There are virtually no deductions in the Tax Code for benefits for Sole-Proprietors. Therefore, some type of incorporation is not only helpful to limit personal liability – to protect the business owner's home and personal property from lawsuits and attachments – but it is essential for any business owner wishing to take advantage of the tax deductions offered to incorporated business owners to provide employee benefits in the Tax Code.

In <u>IRS Publication 535 on Business Expenses</u>, there are a number of substantial employee benefits that Owner-Employees can take advantage of, including the following:

- Accident and Health Plans
- Adoption Assistance
- Cafeteria Plans
- Dependent Care Assistance
- Educational Reimbursement Plans
- Life Insurance Coverage
- Welfare Benefit Funds

<u>Publication 535</u> also offers a dozen other insurance deductions for small businesses. These deductible insurance premiums are for:

- Loss Insurance
- Credit Insurance
- Group Hospitalization and Medical Insurance
- Liability Insurance
- Malpractice Insurance
- Workers' Compensation Insurance
- Contributions to a State Unemployment Insurance Fund
- Disability and Overhead Insurance
- Car and other Vehicle Insurance
- Life Insurance
- Business Interruption Insurance

These premium deductions are in addition to the other business expense deductions provided by Section 162(a) of the Code. In general, Section 162(a) allows a deduction for all ordinary and necessary expenses paid or incurred in the carrying on of a trade or business. Specifically, Treasury Regulations Section 1.162-10(a) provides that:

> Amounts paid or accrued within the taxable year for … a sickness, accident, hospitalization, medical expense… welfare, or similar benefit plan, are deductible under Section 162(a) if they are ordinary and necessary expenses of the trade or business.

The biggest and best known deductions in the Tax Code are for life insurance and for contributions to welfare benefit plans. In fact, in confirming that Section 162(a) and Reg. Section 1.162-10(a) authorize the deductibility of an employer's contribution to an employee benefit plan, or so- called "welfare benefit plan" as an ordinary and necessary business expense, Revenue Ruling 69-478 states in explicitly clear language:

> A corporation's nonrefundable contribution to an employees' trust to provide…life insurance for both active and retired employees is deductible under section 162 of the Code.

Additionally, the Treasury Regulations under Section 1.162 provide for no less than five separate categories of deductions for life insurance premiums paid by a business:

1. Reg. §1.162-1 – Business expenses (including management expenses and insurance premiums)
2. Reg. §1.162-7 – Compensation for personal services
3. Reg. §1.162-9 – Bonuses to employees
4. Reg. §1.162-10 – Employee benefits
5. Reg. §1.162-10T – Questions and answers relating to the
   deduction of employee benefits under the Tax Reform Act
   of 1984 (including contributions to a welfare benefit fund)

Along with the "deductible" reasons for utilizing a welfare benefit plan, the many "non-deduction" reasons for a small business to adopt a welfare benefit plan are in some cases even more compelling than just getting the tax deduction. For example, the "non-deduction" reasons for contributing to a welfare benefit plan are as follows:

- Allows employers to provide economic security for their employees on a cost-effective and selective basis;
- Contributions can be made in good times to fund a reserve for
  trying economic times;
- Plan funds are secure from the hands of creditors, personal as
  well as corporate;

- Contributions are unlimited and may vary from year to year
  subject to the "qualified cost";
- Funds inside the plan can accumulate tax free;

- Death proceeds can be received by the next generation income, estate and gift tax free;
- Benefits can be provided on a selective basis;
- No need to provide benefits to rank and file employees;
- There is no vesting of benefits for employees who terminate prematurely;
- Contributions to the plan are not limited by qualified plan rules and will not interfere with the funding of pension, profit-sharing or 401(k) plans;
- Not subject to ERISA rules;
- Not subject to the IRC Section 529 educational benefit plan limits;
- No 10% penalty for "early" or "late" distributions;
- Not subject to Voluntary Employee Benefit Association (IRC Section 501(c)(9))(VEBA) nondiscrimination rules (no post-retirement life insurance may be made available);
- Not limited by VEBA compensation caps;
- Not subject to 419A(f)(6) rules or scrutiny;
- Eventually all contributions made to the Trust will be deductible over time due to the unlimited and automatic carryover provision for excess contributions under IRC Section 419(d);
- Not subject to the "listed" transaction penalties of Section 6707A.

XVII. The Amazing Tax-Deductible 529 Plan

In truth, Section 529 "Qualified Tuition Plans" are not tax-deductible for income tax purposes, but there are educational benefit trusts that are tax deductible and have been around for more than 30 years. You must be an incorporated business or LLC to take advantage of the **business** deduction that a small business would receive for funding the tuition, room, and board of an employee's eligible children (see, e.g., Greensboro Pathology v. United States, 698 F.2d 1196 (1982), and Schneider v. Commissioner, T.C. Memo 1992-24 (1992)). Why would anyone put money into a Section 529 Plan where there is no tax deduction, no freedom of investment like a CRT, and there are penalties when you try to take the money out for anything other than college expenses, even in an emergency?

Even worse, the Section 529 plan has all sorts of rules and limits for money going in – and any amounts over $13,000 per year are considered to be taxable gifts. So, no income tax deduction and anything above $13,000 a year causes a Gift Tax, yet Americans put billions and billions a year into their own state's 529 plan despite it being a total rip-off to the consumer and only makes huge commissions for the Wall Street firms that run them.

And perhaps worst of all, there is no downside protection in the typical 529 plan. If the President can lose 37-39% in one year in **his** 529 plan for his two children, who do you think is going to look out for you, the SEC? During the stock market downturn of 2008 and 2009, the President's 529 plan lost as much as 39%. The President would have been much better off with an equity-indexed annuity that gives you most of the market appreciation when the stock market goes up, but then protects you from having a downside drop when the market falls 20, 30, or even 40%. In fact, most annuities or equity-indexed universal life insurance plans will credit you with 1 or 2% no matter how much the market falls.

So, you can use a welfare benefit plan in your newly incorporated Delaware corporation or LLC that has no limits on contributions and no penalties on withdrawals or distributions, or you can stay with the non-deductible 529 plan that creates a Gift Tax problem for you on contributions over $13,000. If you do not incorporate, you would be better off with equity-indexed universal life insurance on your own rather than an expensive and inflexible 529 plan.

XVIII. How to Bulletproof Your Tax Return

We recommend that all taxpayers file two disclosure forms. The first, Form 8275, protects you from penalties assessed on any deduction you take as a business expense, and the second, Form 8886, protects you from the Draconian, unconscionable, and unconstitutional penalties contained in Sections 6662A, 6707A, and 6708 among others created by the AJCA of 2004.

By filing the Form 8275, you do not increase your changes of being audited, but in fact decrease your chances of being audited and, should you be audited, you increase your chances of winning the audit because you have already done your homework and exhibited that you had "reasonable cause" and "good faith" to take the deduction and "substantial authority" to back up the deduction.

Your chances of being audited are determined by the IRS computer, by comparing your return, income, and deductions to that of all the other taxpayers filing in your category. This computer analysis is called the "DIF" factor, which stands for the Discriminant Inventory Function System.

Let us assume your return is "picked" for audit by the IRS computer. The protective filing of Form 8275 helps you in at least three ways:

1. It protects you from any assessment of penalties should you lose the argument over the deduction;

2. When the IRS hand-screens your tax return because it was selected for audit by the DIF score, the IRS auditor might immediately understand why the computer picked you out because you had a $50,000 property casualty loss due to your summer house burning down, thus saving you from an expensive and extensive audit.

3. Because you have done your homework and your tax professional has already done the research and put together the substantial authority for you in advance, and perhaps even prepared an opinion letter on the issue for you, when it comes time for the actual audit your tax professional will be completely prepared to argue your case. Eighty to ninety percent of the time, your tax professional will win the audit right then and there because you have fully disclosed and fully defended your tax position. Usually, the IRS auditor will back down on the big claim that is fully substantiated and instead go after some minor expense to justify the time spent on the audit.

There is no downside to filing a protective Form 8275, which is not to be confused with a Form 8275**R**, which is for tax shelters and other unorthodox deductions that the Treasury does not approve of or is contrary to IRS and Treasury rules and regulations. Filing this form may not trigger an audit – though some believe it will – but you would be crazy to use any type of frivolous or fraudulent tax scheme when there are so many **legitimate** ways to get tax deductions and avoid taxes playing by the Government's own rules. The IRS regularly posts on its website the latest frivolous tax shelter schemes going around the Country. Do not be suckered into one of those schemes.

The instructions for the Form 8886 even expect you to file what is known as a "protective" disclosure, because there is so much controversy over "listed transactions" and there are so many normal transactions that may someday be deemed by the IRS to be "substantially similar" to a "listed transaction" several years after the fact. Because the tax penalties are so high – in the hundreds of thousands – and the avenues of appeal so limited, it is just plain crazy not to file a protective disclosure form.

The Form 8886 should definitely be filed with all Section 412(e) pension plans and all small business welfare benefit plans using life insurance because of IRS Notice 2009-59 that added welfare benefit plans using life insurance as a funding vehicle to their list of "listed" transactions. Until Congress gets rid of these unconscionable and unconstitutional penalties, you and your tax professional need to protect **you** with this simple disclosure form on a **protective** filing basis only. It eliminates the penalties and a lot of headaches later.

XIX. The Tax-Free Bridge

"Where I live in Alexandria, Virginia, near the Supreme Court building there is a toll bridge across the Potomac River. When in a rush, I pay the toll and get home early. However, I usually drive outside the downtown section of the city, and cross the Potomac on a free bridge. If I went over the toll bridge and through the toll without paying, I would be guilty of tax evasion. However, if I go the extra mile and drive outside the city of Washington to the free bridge, I am using a legitimate, logical and suitable method of tax avoidance. And, I am providing a useful social service as well. For my tax evasion, I should be punished. For my tax avoidance, I should be commended. **_The tragedy of life today is that so few people know that the free bridge even exists_**_." – Supreme Court Justice Louis Brandeis on Legitimate Tax Avoidance*

"There are two systems of taxation in our country: one for the informed and one for the uninformed."
– Judge Learned Hand

"The legal right of the taxpayer to decrease the amount of what otherwise would be his taxes, or altogether avoid them, by means which the law permits, cannot be doubted."
– <u>Gregory v. Helvering</u>, 293 U.S. 465 Supreme Court (1935)

"Over and over again Courts have said that there is nothing sinister in so arranging one's affairs as to keep taxes as low as possible. Everybody does so, rich or poor; and all do right, for nobody owes any public duty to pay more than the law demands." *– <u>Commissioner v. Newman</u>, 159 F.2d 848,850-51 (2d Cir. 1947)*

BOOK II
CHANGE AMERICA

*"Every nation has the Government
that it deserves."*

- Joseph de Maistre, quoting Voltaire

XX. Balanced Budget Amendment

The biggest threat America faces is the $13 trillion deficit of our own making. It makes no sense to blame the President, because Congress is in charge of two things: Revenue (Taxes) and Spending. President Clinton handed over a budget surplus that was created by the excellent decision of Senator Bob Dole and President Bush (41) to raise taxes somewhat to take care of the first war in Iraq and the Bank Bailout caused by the Savings and Loan crisis and the RTC – Resolution Trust Corporation, a predecessor to TARP that was done correctly. Although the decision to raise taxes probably cost him the 1992 election, President George Bush (41) will go down in history as one of the best presidents of all time. Sad to say, President Bush (43) will not fare so well. Despite the scandals during the Clinton years, it was the combination of a Balanced Budget created by Senator Dole and President Bush (41), and the fiscal conservatives that joined Congress in 1994 that led to America's unparalleled prosperity from 1994-2000. We now have the chance to regain that same prosperity again with the return of control of Congress to the Republicans, a centrist progressive liberal President with a strong wife, and increased revenue with the sunset of the Bush Tax Cuts. Hopefully, this time we will get it right, and the Republican-controlled Congress will waste no time on impeachment, abortion, gun control, and the Defense of Marriage Act, but rather assure America's future with reforms to Social Security, Medicare, and the way Congress does business.

If nothing is done, and interest rates on our National IOU's (our bond debt) rise to 6-7%, the interest alone on the debt will be more than our Gross National Product – forget the tax revenues received by the Treasury. Even if we tax all of the rich at 100%, we will not be able to pay our debts as a country and this is without paying back a penny of principal on the debt. The only way out will be to print more money, devalue the dollar, and destroy our economy for a generation or two.

The deficit time bomb is ticking and if some type of mandatory fiscal restraint is not placed on Congress, we will self-destruct. The only way to guarantee that Congress is restrained is with a Balanced Budget Amendment. Most state governors need to abide by a Balanced Budget clause in their constitutions, and we came close to passing a Balanced Budget Amendment in Congress. Once it passes Congress, it will easily win passage in the necessary 37 states.

XXI. Restore the Line Item Veto

Most governors have some version of the Line Item Veto. The Line Item Veto would give the President the chance to strike all of the "earmarks" that were formerly referred to as political "pork" that routinely appear now in each of the 1,000 page Bills that come out of Congress. If the President wants a Christmas tree passed by Congress, then he is helpless and must accept each and every ornament that Congress places on the tree.

Congress tried to remedy this and restore the President's legitimate veto power with the Line Item Veto Act of 1996, which was short lived and ruled unconstitutional by a 6-3 ruling by the Supreme Court in Clinton v. New York, 524 U.S. 417 (1998). Sad to say it was Republican Rudy Giuliani that opposed the Line Item Veto. To be sure, there is nothing whatsoever unconstitutional about the Line Item Veto. The penalties under IRS Sections 6662A, 6707A, and 6708 created by the AJCA of 2004 though, are entirely unconstitutional. Armed commando raids by the IRS-CID on totally innocent homes and small businesses based on sealed search warrants – that is unconstitutional. But the Line Item Veto? Just a cursory reading of The Federalist Papers will convince anyone that the Founders all favored some form of checks and balances on a fiscally out-of-control Congress – as we have now.

99

There is virtually no chance that Congress will police itself and end all earmarks. Basically, the only part of a 1,000 page bill that most members of Congress read is the earmark provision that they snuck in to benefit some constituent of theirs. Whether it is a Senator or a Congressman, Republican or Democrat, they all play the earmark game and all are expected to bring home the bacon – or "pork" as it were. There is no chance Congress will end earmarks on their own, so the resurrection of a version of the Line Item Veto is a necessity to save America from the deficit abyss it faces.

Although there is a very good chance that the old "Line Item Veto" would be found constitutional by the new Supreme Court, it makes sense to change several items in the legislation to make it more palatable to the Supreme Court. Remember the original Line Item Veto Act was proposed by a Republican Congress and signed by a Democratic President. The leading opponent of the Line Item Veto at the time was Senator Byrd of West Virginia, who has passed away, and the sponsor of the original bill was Arizona Senator and recent Presidential candidate, John McCain, who is very much alive and concerned about out-of-control Congressional spending.

There are several easy ways to modify the original Line Item Veto legislation to appease the Supreme Court. But more importantly, America needs to vote Republican in the election of November 2010 to set the stage for the return of fiscal restraint to Congress. There is no hope of tax relief until the deficit is brought down. There is no hope of bringing the deficit down until spending is brought under control. Spending by Congress will not be controlled without some form of Balanced Budget Amendment and Line Item Veto legislation.

XXII. Save Social Security

Depending on whom you believe, Social Security will be bankrupt in 2028 or 2038, if it is not already. Many commentators refer to Social Security as the greatest "Ponzi" scheme of all time. Thanks to Bernie Madoff, everyone now knows what a "Ponzi" scheme really is. Actually, Charles Ponzi was doing a better job for his investors than the Government is doing for our elderly, and without the Government's imprimatur, the proponents, organizers, and administrators of Social Security would have been indicted for Federal mail and wire fraud years ago.

What can a Republican Congress really do about Social Security? First and foremost, do **not** talk about privatization. People like the Government guarantee. Most Senators and Congressmen view Social Security as the "third rail" of American politics – to touch it is to die. But everyone knows it needs to be reformed, so here is how to do it:

1. All people born after 2012 will receive full Social Security at Age 80 only and reduced amounts beginning at age 70. Payments at age 62 and 65 are nonsensical for this generation. The next generation will easily live to age 90, and the generation yet unborn will reach age 100.

If Willard Scott survives, the entire Today Show will be dedicated to people making the century mark.

2. All people becoming citizens after 2012 will waive receiving any Social Security benefits. Whether it is a PhD math wiz from India working for Microsoft or a Mexican migrant laborer – open up the doors. They will legally still pay FICA and FUTA, but they will receive no benefits.

3. Use Al Gore's "Lock Box" approach, but call it a "Trust Fund." "Lock Box" is a bad investment setup at a bank so that the money goes directly to the bank in order to secure a loan or accounts receivable financing. A "Trust Fund" on the other hand is a good thing. Everyone would secretly like to be a "trust fund baby" and know that there is money being set aside for them. Right now Social Security has no assets other than low interest IOU notes from the Government. When the Government starts printing more paper and notes to "monetize" its debt away, Social Security recipients will be the hardest hit and have no time to prepare.

Everything is worth less and costs more when the dollar goes down in value. It has happened to other countries, it can happen to us.

4. Invest only in the Preferred Stocks and Bonds of American companies. Imagine what would happen if we treated Social Security like the endowment fund at Yale and Harvard. Appoint a Board of two dozen fund advisors to monitor the Social Security Fund and invest in only the Preferred Stocks, Bonds, and Capital Trust instruments of America's 1,000 largest companies. With those simple parameters, even the most conservative fund manager could easily earn 8%. Capital preservation is the primary goal and there is no need to keep up with the S&P 500 or other fund managers. No investments in timber, oil, or rare paintings like other national funds do. Then imagine when the Trust Fund issues its own 5-year and 10-year bonds at 2% and 3% and invests the funds at 8%. That is more than leverage: that is positive arbitrage. The Trust Fund will be solvent forever.

5. Since the new Social Security Trust Fund will be invested in the American economy and American business, it will

be a great shot in the arm. It will be a positive long-term injection of new money to fuel American business. Unlike the Government stimulus that helped **no** American businesses, small or large, by investing in the bonds, capital trusts, and preferred stocks of America's best companies, those companies can send more orders to their vendors and those vendors need to hire more workers to fill the large order they just got from Acme Steel, Acme Express, or Acme Electric. That would create a true "trickle-down" effect.

6. There is no need for "needs" testing. It is too controversial and will never pass anyway. A much better idea is to make all of Social Security taxable. If someone has no pension or a meager pension, then they will pay no tax. If they have a "fat-cat" pension like most Congressmen and Government workers do, then they will have to pay taxes on it. Thus, the people who really need Social Security get it and keep 100%, while those who are well off and do not need it will give 40% back to the Government in the form of taxes.

7. Farm out the administration of Social Security to ADP or MetLife. ADP is America's largest payroll processor and could easily handle processing Social Security checks as well as payroll checks. MetLife is one of America's biggest insurance carriers and processes pension checks for millions of Americans. At the time this is written, none of us own any ADP or MetLife stock, but both would be good investments for the new Social Security Trust Fund. Warren Buffett became rich by investing in American companies, while Social Security is going broke investing in Government bonds. Go figure. By privatizing the administration of Social Security, the Government could save the taxpayers billions of dollars a year in salary, health insurance and pension benefits for the thousands of people who work in the Social Security office and make double or triple what the administration people at ADP or MetLife make.

XXIII. Privatize the Administration of Medicare and Medicaid

It is simply beyond belief that the same Government that feels

that it needs to hire private contractors (e.g., Halliburton, Blackwater,

n.k.a. Xe) to fight the war in Iraq, or Delta Airlines to provide transport

for the troops, or even Boeing to make the planes or Dell to make the

computers, feels that it is perfectly capable to operate and administer

the largest "free" medical insurance system in the World. Each year,

American taxpayers lose $50-80 billion in fraud and over $100 billion

in wasteful payments through Medicare (Does every elderly person

really need a motorized wheelchair or scooter?). The outright fraud is

so pervasive in America that the CBS show 60 Minutes has done three

separate episodes on Medicare fraud and the problems of catching or

stopping the crooks.

If Aetna or United Health Care were to be in charge, fraud would

be brought down to a bare minimum. All of the false billing would

stop immediately, or the crooks would be exposed and prosecuted very

quickly. If a *bona fide* claim was accidentally denied – one call to an

attorney or a Congressman would take care of that. More importantly,

90% of the waste comes in the last six months of life **because no one**

wants to pull the plug on Grandma. So every possible miracle drug or procedure is tried and tested to keep Grandma alive. We can prolong life artificially for years – all at the taxpayer's expense and with no oversight by anyone. The doctors and hospitals all approve because the unchecked medical expenses go directly to their bottom line; even after <u>60 Minutes</u> did an excellent exposé on the millions wasted in the last six months of life per terminally ill patient. No one wants to be on the wrong side of a Terry Schiavo "pull the plug" decision that foolishly went all the way to Congress rather than trusting the advice of doctors, the husband's wishes, or even the decisions by the Florida Courts. If the Mother and Father wanted to take over their daughter's medical bills while she remained in a vegetative state – never to recover – there probably would have been no debate of the issue. But what happens when the insurance is exhausted, the family funds are exhausted, and the Husband is facing bankruptcy? The question of the "Right to Life" quickly changes to a question of the "Quality of Life" to the question of "Who Pays?" There is no current cost control on Medicare and/ or Medicaid for the last months of life where 60-80% of the costs are depending on the patient and the ailment.

If only the administration of Medicare and Medicaid was done by the private sector, families would have a doctor or nurse that they could talk to who would advise them on what to do with Grandma at the end of her life. Most people would want to die painlessly and gracefully at home in their bed with the help of a local hospice. No rational person would want to be permanently left in a vegetative state, kept alive by a breathing machine and chained to a hospital bed by electrodes and feeding tubes. In the Government-run program, there is no calculation of the cost controls or options for a better quality of life, and there is nothing that stops the waste in the system or the outright theft from the program.

Ironically, the Government has setup its own website to combat Medicare fraud called: www.stopmedicarefraud.gov, where it proudly claims in a press release from the US Department of Justice Strike Force that its HEAT (Health Care Fraud Prevention and Enforcement Action Team) has helped in obtaining indictments of more than 810 individuals who have falsely billed Medicare for more than $1.85 billion. Some 500 of the 810 have been convicted, but at what expense? At a million dollars per trial; that is $500 million. Even if the person pled guilty, sending them to jail costs the Government $50,000 per year for the three to five year sentence. Had they been snorting cocaine with a black or Hispanic teenager in Boston, they would have received at least a ten year sentence. More importantly, stopping $2 billion of fraud in three years when it is estimated there is $80-100 billion in Medicare fraud **each year** seems to be a useless effort. But notice there is no discussion of stopping the hundreds of billions in Medicare waste over the same three years. In fact, the Government website, "www.stopmedicarefraud.gov," has links to other sites to apply for benefits, a Government grant, or even a job with the Government.

Obviously, the privatization of the **administration** of Medicare, Medicaid, and other Government Health Care programs will immediately curtail fraud because private insurance carriers have systems in place to double check each and every claim made before it is paid. And if a carrier becomes too stingy, it will be remedied by a call to a Congressman, hopefully a Republican Congressman, or to a law firm. Either way, the claim dispute will be settled quickly by the private carrier, because it is not their money, and if the "boss" – the Government – wants the claim paid, the claim will be paid.

The major difference will be that the Government could let go a lot of people in the Health and Medical Services Department, the Central Management Services (CMS) Department, and the offices of Health and Human Services. As much as 99% of the fraud will be gone, but now we can professionally begin to analyze and curtail waste in the Medicare program. Nothing on the Government's website talks about the curtailment of waste. Remember, the President's Health Care Reform Bill cuts over $500 billion from Senior citizens over a period of five years. If the Fraud unit has only found $2 billion in fraud in three years, and there is no analysis of waste, much less talks to control and curtail waste, that means the President will cut real flesh and bone from Senior benefits, not just fat, pork, fraud, and waste. There is nothing to fear from privatizing the administration of Medicare and Medicaid. The Government will still fund the program, but now there can be a serious effort to cut waste and fraud.

XXIV. Deregulate Health Care

Why would there be a provision in the President's Health Care "reform" bill to regulate the buying and selling of gold? What does the buying or selling of gold coins or gold bullion have to do with healthcare? Nothing, of course. But then again everyone hates the President's Health Care Bill, and the Democrats that voted for the bill should all be voted out of office for not reading, much less understanding the significant burden they just put on doing small business in America.

Section 9006 of the Patient Protection and Affordable Care Act of 2010 (PACA) creates a new Tax Code Section 6041(h) that requires individuals and small businesses to report any expenditure of $600 or more with a single vendor. There are no positive comments on this Section of PACA and the negative commentators are legion. Most commentators are remarking on how small businesses will need to account for their weekly expenditures at Staples or computer purchases at Dell – not to mention Apple – and even the purchase of a new tractor from John Deere. The purveyors of gold coins are up in arms saying this is just the first step so that the IRS-CID agents can come to bust into your house to confiscate your gold. No one from Congress is going on the Sunday morning talk shows to say that this is a ridiculous conspiracy theory made up by Glenn Beck. The silence is deafening and Glenn Beck is looking more and more like a prophet rather than the right wing nut job the Left would like to portray him to be.

The original purpose of the IRS Form 1099 was to report services of $600 or more, especially if **you**, as the small business, wanted the tax deduction for paying that $600. Now, beginning January 1, 2012, if you spend over $600 with any vendor, they expect the **buyer** – meaning you – to report the transaction for anything. So the small business that spends $600 or more at Staples must report that. Office supplies are tax deductible, of course. And to prove that tax deduction, you would just use your company credit card to prove the deduction. No Form 1099 is needed.

So why does Congress want a record of **your** purchases? Well, a Congressman would tell you that when you sell your old car to your neighbor for $5,000, you don't report the transaction and you keep the $5,000 cash tax-free. Your neighbor reports the transaction at $1,000 when he registers the car in his name so he pays only $80 in sales tax rather than $400. So, Congress thinks this will help it raise $17 billion in taxes to pay for the President's Trillion Dollar Health Care Bill (PACA). Does that mean American families will have to report the $600 they spend at McDonald's, or the beer and cigarettes they buy from Budweiser and Altria? Apparently so. There are no exceptions. The small business that spends $100 a week on pizzas for employees lunches will need to report that – whether the lunch is deductible or not.

None of this makes any sense – other than it is the single greatest intrusion on the private life of most Americans since – well…the beginning of the Country in 1776, when the people did not like the way they were being treated by King George. This is where the Gold Bugs come in – to explain the rationale for the Government's move. When President Roosevelt outlawed the ownership of gold, it signaled all sorts of tyrannical conspiracies. Those conspiracy theorists have come out of the closet and they are starting to make a lot of sense.

Now many historians believe America's zenith was with President Coolidge and Andrew Mellon at the helm. Many arch-conservatives hate FDR and the New Deal, but the "safety net" of John Rawls and other authors would have come into the American culture over time because it just makes sense. But when Americans must sacrifice their liberty and their freedoms to supposedly help to provide the "safety net" for other less well off Americans, then there is something wrong with the system.

This is what the gold coin dealers and the Gold Bugs realize. Since there is no deduction when you buy gold coins for your own asset protection or financial planning reasons (even Jim Cramer recommends to buy gold coins or gold stocks or the ETF GLD), the Government must force the **Buyer** to report the transaction, and the Government will have the names and addresses of all those Americans who are putting their faith in gold rather than the US Dollar. Since the

President's Health Care Bill PACA passed, gold has hit and surpassed its all time high, and the Dollar is at its lows for the year.

During this election cycle, no Democrat running for office has come forward to defend this new IRS Tax Code Section that will dramatically impair your ability to do business – and mind your own business and privacy. This new Tax Code Section is the single greatest threat to American privacy and liberty since the Republic was formed. Yet only so-called "crack pots" like Ron Paul (hates the Fed) and Glenn Beck (hates the President and most liberals), and talk show hosts like the distinguished jurist Judge Napolitano or well-represented Forbes Magazine publisher Steve Forbes are talking about this intrusive invasion by the IRS into a **nondeductible** area. Remember, if you buy gold coins as a collector – you do not get a deduction. If you as the buyer report that you bought more than $10,000 in gold coins, could it be so that you could use those coins to facilitate your drug buying business? If you took out $10,000 or more from a bank in cash, you and the bank would fill out a form. Just for fun, take out $11,000 from one bank and then deposit $11,000 in cash into a different bank. Wait until you see the looks you get and the forms you will be asked to fill out – and ask for a copy of the report the bank will do on you that they will send to the Government.

Not only will this new law interfere with your ability to do gold deals, it will also interfere with your ability to buy and sell the Government's other favorite obsession – guns. Buying an expensive rifle will require you to report that you bought the rifle, even if you did not register it with the local authorities, or you will be forced to join the "underground economy" or the "grey" market. Just for our Evangelical Christian audience, and to make sure that this terribly offensive and intrusive law does not go unnoticed at election time, and to support the efforts of great Americans like former New York Governor George Pataki who are trying to overturn and repeal PACA and the President's wrong minded Health Care Reform Bill, remember it is Section 9006 of PACA that creates a new Code Section 6041(h) that requires everyone to report total transactions with anyone over $600. Also remember that in the Bible, no one could buy or sell without the mark of the Beast, and the number of the Beast is 666. Historically "666" represents Nero Caesar in both Greek and Hebrew, but this violation of American freedoms and liberty is far more frightening (and real) than any possible Antichrist.

So what should real healthcare reform look like? First, healthcare really means insurance coverage. As such, we should get the Government out of the medical insurance business just like it got out of the regulating the auto insurance business, and has never been in the phone business.

Second, there needs to be the ability to buy insurance across state lines, without that it is easy for the "BUCA monsters" to have a monopoly in the individual states. BUCA stands for the **B**lue Cross Carriers, **U**nited Healthcare, **C**IGNA, **A**etna, and their various affiliates and subsidiaries. Wellpoint and Anthem are examples of Blue Cross companies that went private, non-tax exempt, and then public.

Third, Congress needs to authorize Association Health Plans so small businesses can join together in IRS Section 419A(f)(6) health plans to increase coverage and access to healthcare at a lower cost.

Fourth, ERISA already allows individual employers to set their own benefits for their own member-employees. The MEWA rules must be changed to allow several employers to join together to do the same.

Fifth, without the ability of small employers to set their own benefits, no reduction in cost is ever possible because the real cost of health insurance is in the 20-30 mandates required by each state. If ERISA or Federal law does not allow employers to ignore the state mandates, a small business will have only a choice between two or three carriers at the same exorbitant price.

Sixth, the big cost of modern healthcare – a.k.a. insurance coverage – is the extra testing and extra unnecessary procedures done by doctors and hospitals to protect themselves from frivolous lawsuits. Since doctors must routinely pay hundreds of thousands of dollars for malpractice insurance, the insurance companies pay for that in the higher costs for more benefits and procedures. Thus, without tort reform helping doctors and hospitals save money on malpractice insurance, there can be no reduction in healthcare costs. If nothing else, we can adopt the "loser pays for the winner's legal fees" system that they have in England.

Seventh, there needs to be an optional Federal licensing program for insurance companies, just as there is for HMOs.

Eighth, employers must be allowed to purchase and provide Mini-med and scaled down versions of health insurance for their employees. Eighty percent of the American workforce can be taken care of with a "Mini-med" policy that costs only $80 a month.

Ninth, the Government should setup a Catastrophic Risk Pool – open to everyone.

Tenth, the only Government plan that makes sense is to have the Government provide a voucher for poor people to get the insurance they need from the lowest cost provider.

XXV. The War Powers of Congress

Most Americans wrongly believe that it is the President that has the power to declare war. Actually, only Congress has the power to declare war and decide whether to fund an ongoing war. As depicted excellently in the book and the film *Charlie Wilson's War*, a couple of well-positioned and right-minded Congressmen can have the Afghans and Osama bin Laden working for us to defeat the Russians in Afghanistan. A part of our history that most Americans do not understand or know anything about is the high watermark of American diplomacy. Somehow we blew it, and the rest of the World knows us only for Vietnam, Iraq, and a new superpower trapped in the quagmire that is Afghanistan. Apparently Americans never learn from history. Just as Donald Trump has had the Miss Universe pageant in Vietnam – 20 years from now he will host it in Baghdad.

After 9/11, everyone wanted to attack Afghanistan. See for example the unforgettable and tragic story of Pat Tillman who gave up a lucrative career in football to die in the hills of Afghanistan – a victim of friendly fire and a massive cover-up. Looking back, President Bush (43) should have hit the mountains of Tora Bora in Afghanistan with the "Shock and Awe" campaign that he hit Iraq with. If we did not get Osama bin Laden then, the chances are he died a natural death somewhere in the hills of Pakistan. Whatever happened to him, dead or alive, he is no longer doing anything to hurt us, but we create more willing martyrs in Afghanistan every day with our presence there. We are doing so many things wrong in Afghanistan that we should seriously reconsider what is going on and what we are doing there. And is the specter of Osama bin Laden being kept alive just like Big Brother would do in George Orwell's *"1984"*?

We nearly bankrupted ourselves in Iraq. Why? What for? Hillary Clinton voted for the war just so she would not be seen as soft on defense. The irony is that she would be the President today if she had truly opposed the war. As for John Kerry, well, as we all now know, he was for the war before he was against it and you should never second-guess yourself or reconsider your original thinking if you want to be President.

Take the case of Larry Lindsey, one of the brightest economic advisors in the Bush (43) White House and former Chairman of the National Economic Council. When he questioned the price tag of the War in Iraq as being too high at $200 million, he was politely shown the door. Not only would he have been a perfect replacement for Greenspan – as he was a well-respected Federal Reserve Governor – he would have stopped the profligate spending that led to the deficit and would have sounded the alarm three years earlier on AIG and the sub-prime mortgage crisis.

Now that the war in Iraq has cost us a trillion dollars and the rebuilding effort is far from over, does anyone realize that to pay for all of the disabled veterans from that war into the future may cost another $500 million, or even as much as $800 million? The money is already committed because no Congressman would be stupid enough or callous enough to vote against a disabled Marine receiving VA benefits. As Abraham Lincoln memorably said during his Second Inaugural Address following the Civil War and that has been our obligation for this Country ever since: "...to care for him who shall have borne the battle and for his Widow and his orphan."

What do we have to show for our trillion dollar expenditure? Not much. What about the decision to go into Baghdad? President Bush (41) and his advisors look like geniuses in stopping short – worried about what would happen to the region with a divided Iraq.

Many of us favor a separate and independent Kurdistan in the North and a separate state in the South, but that is for another book. The big mistake that was made in the Iraq campaign was disbanding the Iraqi army. All 400,000 well-trained soldiers sent home to think about who they should blame for being out of a job and for invading their homeland. Imagine if someone conquered America and disbanded the 82nd Airborne. Whoever did that would certainly not be safe in the woods and hills of North Carolina. Yet no one thinks about that in Iraq? We formerly supported the Shah in Iran, why couldn't we support one of our cronies to take over as an interim leader in Iraq?

Because the guy we wanted was accused of taking bribes and we alienated the other natural leaders.

The point of this should be clear. We have nearly bankrupted ourselves in two unpopular wars that made no sense in either case. Even if you supported both wars – you have to admit mistakes were made, money and lives were wasted, and Charlie Wilson would have done a much better job with some well-placed CIA operatives working with local natural leaders. We could have been the "Lafayette" to some Iraqi or Afghan "George Washington." Instead, we are wasting our valuable financial resources and the precious little political capital we have left in the World. Notice "Al Qaeda" has not attacked China or Russia.

Finally, why do we have troops spread out all over the World? We waste over $100 billion a year on having troops in England, Germany, Japan and Korea to name just a few of our more than 50 foreign posts. If China decides to invade Taiwan, would we really rush to Taiwan's defense? But why should China do that? They took over Hong Kong without firing a shot and that one move spurred China's rise as an economic superpower. Everyone is already proclaiming China the winner, and we in America did not even hear the starting gun. China and Russia are not wasting money on foreign outposts. Clearly both have their respective political problems in Tibet and Chechnya and Georgia, but no one is telling them what to do or not do. No one dares. We are too afraid to take "Most Favored Nation" status away from China, much less attack them. So why have troops in Korea or Japan? So they can be killed by an out-of-control North Korean dictator? The only nuclear warhead missile that North Korea has will only reach as far as American bases in Korea or Japan. They certainly will not attack China. Suffice it to say, our entire foreign policy is a riddle wrapped in a mystery inside an enigma, as Churchill would say. It is terribly misguided at best and suicidal at worst.

Here is wisdom for those who understand it. Instead of closing down Gitmo – Guantanamo Bay in Cuba – make it a model modern military prison. Give everyone real, American, trials there – not in the center of New York City. Let's normalize relations with Cuba. We fought to keep Elian Gonzalez here – let's open the door to other Cubans. And how about this: let's buy all of Cuba's sugarcane to make ethanol like Brazil does – out of sugarcane and not corn – so we can become energy independent just like Brazil has done. Ethanol from corn is a bad deal because corn is an important food for animals, so higher corn prices affect all food prices from cereal to beef. Castro admits that his style of government is not working, and the truth is – neither is ours.

The Constitution vests the War Powers in Congress, not the President. We need someone in Congress to stand up, as Charlie Wilson did, and say "I have a better idea – a better way of getting the job done." If we let Joe Kennedy buy all of Venezuela's oil cheaply for our senior citizens, and Cuban sugar makes us less dependent on Arab oil, this will be a much better World. When Steven Wynn opens a new casino in Havana and Bruce Springsteen and Bon Jovi play there, we will know that Papa Hemingway has returned and all is right with the World. It will be good for the whole World when a portion of Havana is referred to as "little Miami" or Nueva Miami as in "new" Miami.

XXVI. Stop Feeding the Beast

If every small business in America would just incorporate and take advantage of one or two of the tax saving ideas described in Book One, we would accomplish the goal that has eluded Washington, i.e., getting money out of Washington and into the hands of American consumers so they can spend. The more they spend, the better the economy. The more that Washington taxes us – the less we have to spend. The less we have to spend – the worse the economy is and the worse it becomes. The more uncertain the regulatory environment the more likely entrepreneurs will sit on their hands and keep their money in the bank rather than borrow from the bank. Even if they wanted to borrow, they could not as no banks are lending when the banks can borrow at 0% and lend to the Federal Government at 3% or invest in Government backed mortgages at 4% and 5%.

Therefore, it is up to the small businesses of America to take a few lessons from Exxon and structure their affairs so that they legitimately pay no taxes. If everyone did this, a true taxpayer revolution, then we could immediately starve the Beast – Washington – into submission. The allegorical Beast in the Bible is nothing compared to the real Beast in Washington. We can starve the Beast by legitimately restructuring our business affairs to pay less tax. Tax evasion is a crime, but tax avoidance, which is legal, should be America's new favorite sport, not just an avocation but a full-time job and duty for all Americans to keep their money flowing in America and out of the IRS's hands in Washington.

Imagine if every small business buys $5 million of life insurance in a tax-deductible welfare benefit trust for $100,000 a year for five years. If there are a million small businesses that will be dramatically hurt by the end of the Bush tax cuts, let them all contribute just $100,000 a year for five years to benefit themselves and not Washington. See IRS Publication 535 on Business Expenses and fill out Forms 8275 and 8886 to bulletproof your returns.

Now, what will happen? The $500,000 put in a welfare benefit trust over five years will save $200,000 in Federal taxes for the business owner and reduce taxes to Washington by $200 billion. That $200 billion is roughly what the Government has put into AIG, one quarter of TARP, and about equal to the total amount of money the stimulus put into the economy. The difference this time is that the money goes to an insurance carrier that pays a commission to an insurance agent who spends the money on his business expenses and payroll. The insurance carrier invests the money in bonds of top-rated companies and indirectly in the stock of S&P 500 companies through various Equity Index investment strategies. That money flows throughout the economy by being invested in the markets, and that is $500 billion that is directly invested in the American economy.

Best of all, upon the death of the insured entrepreneurs, there is at least $5 trillion payable to the next generation Income, Estate, and Gift Tax free. That amount payable to American families, free from the hands of creditors, equals about half of the outstanding national debt. The purchase of life insurance in a welfare benefit plan serves at least three beneficial goals:

First, it starves the Beast; Second, it puts money into the economy to circulate; and Third, it creates tax-free wealth for future generations of Americans that is secure from the hands of creditors and the IRS for generations to come after that.

XXVII. What Can Congress Really Do?

During the recent televised debates, several Senate candidates were asked whether or not they favored the death penalty. This is a classic example of what is wrong with our political process, as no one in the audience thought the question was strange or out of place. The reporter that asked the question should be assigned to a remedial high school civics class.   Let us be clear, no Congressman or Senator will ever vote on the death penalty, nor will any Congressman or Senator be able to vote on – much less outlaw – abortion. Decriminalizing drugs and legalizing gay marriage will eventually be done on a state-by-state basis; and no member of Congress will ever vote on either of these issues. So what can a member of Congress really do? Well, for starters, he can do his or her job which is to oversee how the billions of the taxpayers' precious, hard-earned dollars are being spent.

There has been no one to say "cut the budget." New offices and positions are opened up each time there is an election. New people come in – but only half of the old people leave. And why leave Government employment when it is steady, pays double what the private sector does, and comes with full health and pension benefits? Obviously, something must be done. Someone has to be the "belt-tightener," and it will never be the newly-elected President. He has too many promises to keep. It has been that way since Andrew Jackson and the "spoils system" and will always stay with us. Therefore, it is up to Congress to end the appropriations (paychecks) for certain departments of the Government. There is no reason for pension benefits for any Government worker. They can have Roth 401(k)s and IRAs like everyone else, but no taxpayer funded retirement. Healthcare should be available, but should be paid for by each Government employee out of his or her paycheck. Obviously the IRS should be cut in half and the Tax Court dissolved. The National Taxpayer Advocate's office can replace the IRS agents, and both the Appeals and the Tax Courts.

Members of Congress should be deficit-cutting vigilantes and insist that the Executive Branch cut all departments across the board by 20%. The Government is bloated and its employees are, for the first time in history, earning double what their private industry counterparts earn. Why would anyone work in the "private" sector if they could have a "no-fire" safe job with the Government that pays twice as much for less work, better conditions, and full pension and health insurance benefits? As if that was not bad enough, recent studies show that thousands of Government employees owe **<u>Billions</u>** in unpaid taxes to the Government, but no IRS-CID commandos are waiting outside of their houses like they did to Denise Simon and her children.

Demand that your Senators and Congressman fight for a balanced budget, cut waste in Medicare and Medicaid, and save Social Security for future generations. Your Senators and Congressman can certainly do something about those issues. Also demand that they reform Congress. Make every bill be available for ten days before it is voted on so that it can be distributed to the press and reviewed by the American people, since it is clear that no one in Congress is reading these thousand page bills written in the dead of night. All of the large bills passed by this current Congress were over a thousand pages, done in the early morning hours, and were not read by anyone in Congress including the Speaker of the House who said, "We will not know what is in the Bill until we vote to pass it." That is no way to run any government. If you vote for a Democratic Congressman, he or she will be forced to vote for the **worst** Speaker of the House that has ever held the office.

For the best example of Congress gone wild, look no further than the repeal of the Glass-Steagall Act that kept the American economy safe for seven decades by separating banks from investment firms, and within the space of a couple of years we had the worst economy since the Great Depression. We have now further compromised our future with the passage of the Dodd-Frank financial "reform". The people responsible for the disaster have destroyed our future. Just bring back Glass-Steagall and regulate the crooks on Wall Street. Remember, the President wants to hire 16,000 new Special Agents to work for the IRS-CID who will kick in your door during an armed assault on your home or small business. On the other hand, there are only 800 people working at the SEC to protect consumers from all of the Ponzi schemes, out of control hedge funds, and firms like Goldman Sachs that pay multi-million dollar fines as if they were traffic tickets without admitting guilt or even fault. After being bailed out by Main Street, Wall Street has just reported a second year of record profits.

An example of a simple act that Congress can do right away to improve the American stock markets is to immediately bring back the "up-tick" rule which prevents the relentless shorting of a stock by requiring that the stock must actually go up before it is shorted again. Without requiring this "up-tick" in value, relentless shorting can destroy a company's value in only a few sessions. Just like Glass-Steagall, the "up-tick" rule has served us well since the Great Depression. Congress should force the SEC to reinstitute that rule immediately to prevent predatory hedge funds from being able to short a stock out of existence because they do not need to wait for an "up-tick" in price before shorting the stock.

Similarly, Congress is in charge of tax policy – all tax policy. A very simple change in the tax laws will fill the pockets of American taxpayers and reduce all of the ridiculous tax shelters, corporate machinations to reduce taxes, and excess executive compensation: simply make corporate dividends tax deductible. If Congress would just allow America's big companies to deduct their dividends, there would be an immediate return of American prosperity overnight.

Additionally, the flat tax that has not found any traction in Congress for individual taxpayers would be the perfect solution for American business, combined with deductible dividends. Corporate profits would be taxed at a flat rate of 15% with all of the exotic and difficult deductions deleted from the Tax Code.

A simplified Tax Code must start first with the large American corporations that are not paying taxes at all anyway. Reducing corporate rates to 15% and making profits distributed as dividends to shareholders tax deductible will create tax-revenue for the Treasury and jumpstart a moribund economy. Then there can be two tax rates for individual taxpayers – a flat 15% for all types of income for taxpayers making up to $500,000 with limited deductions such as the mortgage deduction for interest on one's house. Above $500,000 of income, all of the tax deductions that taxpayers are normally accustomed to would be allowed, and the flat tax would be at 40%. Small business owners could take advantage of the tax ideas contained in this Book to protect themselves from being over taxed. But, simplification of the Tax Code is something your Congressman can do and should do.

Last but not least, write your Senator and Congressman to work for the repeal of all IRS penalties, especially the Draconian ones like Sections 6707A, 6662A, 6708, and the new frightening Section 6041(h) on the President's Health Care Bill (PACA). Many people running for Congress would like to repeal the President's entire Health Care Bill.

132

But, the idea that no one read the Bill before voting on it means that every Democrat who voted for the Bill with the new intrusive 1099 Form for any expenditure over $600 actually approved an egregious violation of the American taxpayer's individual freedoms and Constitutional rights.

Of all the things your Congressman or Senator can do, they can stop these armed commando raids on American citizens as Senator Patrick Moynihan and Senator Roth thought they had done with the passage of the IRS Restructuring and Reform Act of 1998 and the institution of the Webster Commission to review taxpayer abuse at the hands of the IRS. No one believes the IRS will ever be done away with altogether, but every category of American business is being strangled by IRS regulation and ridiculous tax policies. Only Kafka could appreciate the "guilty until proven innocent beyond a reasonable doubt" investigative power of the IRS coupled with armed commando raids on innocent homes and businesses. To quote the famous KGB leader, Lavrenti Beria: "Show me the man and I will find you the crime."

Your Congressman cannot and should not be used to regulate your neighbor's business, but he should be used to protect you and your family from unwarranted and illegal intrusions into your life by an out-of-control Government.

Instead of regulating you – your Congressman should rein in the out of control spending of the Government, which will only end in the fall of American culture as we know it.

> *"Decency, security and liberty alike demand that government officials shall be subjected to the same rules of conduct that are commands to the citizen. In a government of laws, existence of the government will be imperiled if it fails to observe the law scrupulously. Our Government is the potent, the omnipresent teacher. For good or for ill, it teaches the whole people by its example. Crime is contagious. If the Government becomes a lawbreaker, it breeds contempt for law; it invites every man to become a law unto himself; it invites anarchy."*

Olmstead v. United States, 277 U.S. 438, 485 (1928)

BOOK III
SAVE THE WORLD

"A society that would sacrifice liberty
for security deserves neither."

- Voltaire to his good friend, Benjamin
Franklin, and as quoted by Thomas Jefferson

XXVIII. Asteroids and the Mayan Calendar

The Mayan Calendar either suggests or predicts – depending with whom you discuss the issue – that the World will come to an end on December 21, 2012. Numerous Cable TV shows have dedicated long programs that suggest Nostradamus, the I Ching, and even Isaac Newton's Bible Code all point to the same date. There is no question that scholarly studies have shown all sorts of "end of the world" dates from Nostradamus alone, and to date, predicting the end of the World or counting on it has been a lousy bet. That sad statistic – or even the end of the known World by our own doing or by an asteroid as was done to the dinosaurs millions of years ago – is not the point of this book. We cannot know, predict, or perhaps even prevent the end of the World in 2012 or some other day. But we can take back our country in the election of 2010, because our Country is in a very dangerous place – every bit as dangerous as 1776. Do you really believe that King George treated the Colonists worse than Congress and Washington, D.C. treats its citizens? It is time to wake up. If you do nothing in November 2010, it will not matter what you do in November 2012.

So, for the sake of this discussion, let us assume the Mayans knew what they were talking about and something is going to happen December 21, 2012 that brings the World as we know it to its untimely end. This time it is not so crazy a bet because scientists discovered a small island in the South Pacific 800 miles off the Coast of Chile – and a couple of thousand miles off the Coast of Mexico and Central America where the Mayans lived when they were the dominant culture of North America – which had on it prominent sculptures and monuments dedicated to the Mayan Gods. So what – you say? You can see for yourself how remote the island is and how difficult it would be to get there – and then how difficult it would be to create a huge jaguar-like stone carving on a mountaintop far from your native home by watching the Cable TV show "Apocalypse Island." Now what if you saw the NASA reports in the New York Times tracing the famous eclipse that will happen on December 21, 2012 showing the best viewing spots in the whole World where the line drawn by the New York Times report travels for thousands of miles of ocean on each side of a spot of land in the middle of nowhere. This island is too small to be on any maps and if you track the path of the eclipse viewing line by latitude and longitude – it hits Apocalypse Island dead on.

As if this was not eerie and unsettling enough, there is the transition of Venus and a rare alignment of the planets that happens only once in 10,000 years, and a shifting of stars that happens only every 13,500 years, and it is all happening that month and that tiny remote island is the best seat in the house for all sorts of astronomical wonders. How did the Mayans know this over a thousand years ago? It is not surprising that the NASA rocket scientists know how to track the path of a future eclipse – because the Sun and the Moon move in con-junction like clockwork – which allows us to track the exact minute and hour of high tide and low tide.

The NASA data can be used to plot the future travel of the eclipse – so people can visit exotic places to view it – and this is what the New York Times astronomer is meant to do every Sunday. It is his job to report interesting planets to view at sunrise or meteor showers that can only be seen at 2:00-3:00 in the morning. But how did the Mayans do that a thousand years ago? We will probably never know.

For our purposes, it is not important to know how the Mayans knew that small island would become the best seat for viewing the end of the World or the famous eclipse, but rather that you suspend your natural disbelief, open your mind, and just believe the World – as you know it – ends on December 21, 2012. Now what are you going to do about it?

If you read about the Apocalypse in the Book of Revelations, you will learn the name of the asteroid that will eventually hit Earth and end life as we know it. The name of that asteroid is in the Bible, yet no one talks about it. Each day the Earth is bombarded with small meteorites, and every century or so there is a bigger one that will leave a large crater or destroy the Siberian forest. Every year, the Earth has several near misses by killer asteroids – sure, they are hundreds of thousands of miles off – but space is infinite and the Moon is only

242,000 miles away.

What is not in the Bible though – is the stuff everyone believes and talks about. There is no "Rapture" discussed in the Apocalypse – there is no "Tribulation" – and there certainly is no "Antichrist" mentioned in the Apocalypse. The word "Antichrist" is only found in John I, and it means the "liar" or the "apostate." As for the mark of a Man or the Beast, the "666" refers to Nero Caesar in Greek and in Hebrew. Look at what Nero did to the early Christians – and you don't think that was what John of Patmos was talking about?

The Battle of Armageddon? It has been fought over 40 times throughout history, and the battle in the Book of Revelation either refers to the Roman invasion and the destruction of Jerusalem in John's time, or one of the famous battles of the Crusades to take back Jerusalem from the "Moslems" when all of the Kings of Europe gathered together outside of Jerusalem. Remember King Richard and the other famous Kings of Europe that joined in the Crusades?

What we consider to be the "word of God" has been carefully sculpted over 2,000 years by many men to be politically acceptable and politically expedient by and for the various rulers over time to keep the masses in check by literally putting the "fear of God" into them. If nothing else, Christianity was meant to be a revolutionary movement to create a New Covenant with God. The Old Covenant with God was for Moses and the Jewish people and had Ten Commandments. The New Covenant with God was proscribed by Christ himself and has only two commandments: "Love God with all of your heart; and Love thy neighbor as you would yourself." That is it. Where does anyone see in those words: Thou shalt oppose abortion, or Thou shalt overrule Roe v. Wade, 410 U.S. 113 (1973)?

The time for hatred, bigotry, and prejudice is long passed. If we do not immediately change the path this Country is on – we will destroy ourselves just as certainly as the asteroid predicted in the Bible will destroy us; and that asteroid has a name. Why would St. John the Divine give a name to the asteroid that will destroy Earth but disguise the name of the so-called "Antichrist" to come? Obviously it was because Nero was blaming the Christians for the fires in Rome and feeding them to the lions in the Coliseum. Criticizing a Caesar in those days could easily get you killed or worse. The Battle of Armageddon has already been fought, Jerusalem burned, and the Temple destroyed so that no stone was left standing on another.

To save America and be able to save the World, the "conservative" wing of the Republican Party must change and must change now – NOW – as in immediately, because the November 2010 and November 2012 elections are even more imminent than the Mayan's prediction of the end of the World in December 2012. Let us open up the tent. Be "conservative" where it counts, budget discipline and fiscal responsibility – and for social issues – live and let live – love and let love.

Spend no time on social issues. In the end, it is all nonsense and a total waste of time and energy.

For example, on immigration, we build a fence for hundreds of millions of dollars to keep who out? Al-Qaeda Terrorists? Or hard working Hispanics who yearn for a better life? Why did we fight so hard to prevent Elian Gonzalez from going home to his father in Cuba, and yet we try to keep as many Mexicans out as possible? Does that make sense? Open borders and the free transport of goods and labor makes for prosperous neighbors – look at the European Union. We, on the other hand, discriminate against Mexicans, while we welcome Canadians and Australians with open arms and give them lucrative jobs and Academy Awards. Our drug policies and "war on drugs" have turned Mexico into a dangerous "narco-terrorist" state. Why did we attack Iraq when its neighbor Iran is far more dangerous to our future and they continue to kidnap American citizens? Why are we still in Afghanistan when it is clear that Osama Bin Laden is either dead or living happily in Pakistan?

One last philosophical question: If we have our million soldiers spread out all over the world from Korea to Germany and Iraq to Afghanistan, what Army do we have that can expel the 12 million "illegal" immigrants? Wouldn't it be smarter for the Republican Party to be the party of hard-working people who want to be free and are willing to work for nothing so their children can have a better life? Lincoln "freed" the slaves with the Emancipation Proclamation and 90% or more of Black Americans have consistently voted against the Republicans ever since. Someone, somewhere, should be smart enough to realize that Hispanic-Americans will make perfect, conservative, God-fearing, Catholic-Christian Republicans. Let us not alienate them into the Democratic Party forever as we did with African-Americans, Jewish-Americans, the Irish, and just about every other immigrant group that ever came to this Country after the Mayflower.

Drugs are part of the same exercise in stupidity. The United States Government spends way too much time and money sending Black and Hispanic children to jail for drug offences. The reason that prosecutors use the Federal Law rather than State Law is so that Black and Hispanic youths can be sentenced to ten years for just being in a car with someone who happens to have cocaine. White children found with drugs in their car will get a severe reprimand from a local municipal judge, but black and Hispanic children will be charged and prosecuted as adults in Federal Court and sentenced to five to ten years for having an illegal substance in their car. Sometimes they do not even have a car.

See for example <u>United States v. Jones</u>, 609 F. Supp. 2d 113 (2009), a notorious case in Boston made even more famous by Chief Judge Wolf's scathing condemnation of the prosecutorial misconduct in the case. The Assistant US Attorneys involved were all sent back for remedial training in handling the prosecution of a crime without violating every rule of the prosecutor's code and the Constitutional rights of the accused, such as handing over exculpatory evidence to the defendant's attorney and not creating false evidence or lies against the accused. The gist of the case in <u>Jones</u> comes down to the testimony of a particular Boston police officer that Jones, **who was on a bicycle** (that is correct – no car – no glove compartment), had no reason to run away (in this case – pedal away) from the arresting officer who claims that he knew Jones. As it turns out, Jones did have a weapon in his possession, but everything else was just a lie. Judge Wolf threw the book at the prosecution for their handling of the case – but Jones was still sentenced to six years in a Federal jail for being on his bicycle at the wrong time and the wrong place.

Judge Wolf is also famous for his criticism of the Boston US Attorney's office in February of 2004, stating that the US Attorney, Michael Sullivan, was turning the Federal Courthouse into a "municipal court." Judge Wolf further criticized US Attorney Sullivan for not going after the "real" criminals, i.e., Enron and big company white-collar criminals. This criticism by Judge Wolf is very interesting indeed, when one considers the new book by Harry Markopolos, where he went to the Federal authorities **in Boston** not once, but three times to expose Bernie Madoff as a fraud and his involvement a Ponzi scheme. US Attorney Michael Sullivan (not to be confused with the AUSA Suzanne

Sullivan in the <u>Jones</u> case), was too busy going after Black and Hispanic kids on bicycles to go after real criminals like Bernie Madoff or the other Wall Street bigwigs that almost collapsed our economy with bogus mortgage and auction rate securities. US Attorney Sullivan was a Bush-appointment and a disciple of John Ashcroft and his misguided policies, and does not deserve to be appointed dog warden in a small New England town, but was instead promoted to head the ATF (Alcohol Tobacco and Firearms) Bureau.

Interestingly enough, the vote on his appointment was blocked by another famous Republican – <u>Larry Craig</u>, the Idaho Senator who was arrested for alleged lewd conduct in the men's room of the Minneapolis-St. Paul Airport. For the cost of arresting, prosecuting, and putting in storage for six years a young black man named Jones, your government will easily spend a million dollars. Jones will not come out of this a better man; how about you? And wouldn't society be better off if we took Jones off of his bicycle and sent him to college or even a technical school on a full scholarship and then maybe let him get his law degree from Harvard as the President did, instead of a Federal prison? It costs far less to educate and rehabilitate someone like Jones, rather than to incarcerate him and then someday discuss eliminating him. Too many individuals who oppose freedom of choice for white women, support the death penalty for black men. Imagine if the President had been arrested for smoking marijuana on his bicycle;

would he be President today? Perhaps the President should have a heart-to-heart talk about this issue with his Attorney General before the Attorney General attacks California's new legislation. Thirty years ago America had 200,000 people incarcerated; now that number is nearly 3 million. There is something wrong with that type of increase. We can no longer afford as a nation to send young black men to jail for having what amounts to several packets of sugar or white powder in their backpacks. The Federal sentencing guidelines are ridiculous and have been ruled unconstitutional and effectively thrown out. It is time that the whole system of Federal Justice is overhauled and examined – before **your door** is busted down in the middle of the night based on a secret warrant from a secret court issued under the Foreign Investigation Surveillance Act (FISA) created under the Patriot Act and as executed by "great" "God-fearing" Republicans like John Ashcroft and Michael Sullivan.

One last thing about Michael Sullivan – with all of those Black and Hispanic young men he put away, he never did indict anyone associated with the 9/11 Terror Attack that led to the beginning of the suppression of so many of our freedoms in the so-called "War on Terror." Remember, two of the four planes that attacked America that day took off from Boston's Logan airport. So even though US Attorney Sullivan got Jones and his bicycle off the street, he missed Bernie Madoff and the 9/11 hijackers. See also the <u>USA Today</u> Study naming the

Boston (Massachusetts) District as the worst of the Federal Districts for prosecutorial misconduct (<u>USA Today</u> – Prosecutors' Conduct Can Tip Justice Scales – September 22, 2010).

Finally, Republicans everywhere should abandon all hopes of overturning <u>Roe v. Wade</u>. Waste no more time discussing the issue or making it a litmus test for a Supreme Court Judge. You do not want the Supreme Court in **your** bedroom executing a sealed search warrant issued by a secret court. Because you keep asking for "conservative" judges to overturn <u>Roe v. Wade</u>, you end up with judges who are willing to ignore all of your precious civil rights and Constitutional rights in the name of justice, the Patriot Act, or collecting on a penalty owed to the IRS. If <u>Roe v. Wade</u> was overturned tomorrow, the laws regarding abortion would return to the states. Forget about Utah, Idaho, or Wyoming; do you seriously think that voters in New York or New Jersey will ever "outlaw" abortion? And if they did, do you seriously believe that if Susie from Scarsdale got "knocked-up" accidentally that her parents would not put her on the next flight to Amsterdam where even drugs are legal? To think that the Federal Government can regulate morality any better than state governments can, is absolute lunacy. So for the Republicans to look to nominating only far-right "socially" conservative candidates when what the Country wants and needs is "fiscally" conservative candidates who really do not care what you do or do not do in your bedroom, and would certainly not approve

146

the issuance of a secret sealed warrant by a secret court to invade your bedroom to serve an IRS subpoena or summons. That is not what you were looking for in supporting "social" conservatives, but that is what you will end up with if you don't watch out. You keep thinking "abortion" and you will soon see your house or business raided by armed commandos from the IRS-CID.

In the same waste of time category is the Republican attack on and disdain for members of the Gay and Lesbian community from the Defense of Marriage Act to the "Don't Ask Don't Tell" policy in the military. This type of hypocrisy just shows how hate-filled, prejudicial, and bigoted certain members of the Republican Party can be. The Senate Democrats all voted to repeal "Don't Ask Don't Tell" and not a single Republican Senator voted for it. Why would any member of the GLBT (Gay, Lesbian, Bisexual and Transgender) community vote Republican ever again? More importantly – what did we accomplish with that vote? If you were on a ridge in Afghanistan pinned down by enemy fire, would you seriously start to question the sex, race, or sexual preference of your fellow soldiers? You would probably want as many Black, Gay, Spanish-speaking transsexuals as you could find that could shoot straight – even if they weren't "straight" – to come to your rescue. What other reasons do we have, other than bigotry and prejudice, for continually hurting these people? Gays are known to be fiercely loyal, brave, and tough fighters; sounds like they might make great soldiers, too.

That is also precisely why spending any time on legislation like the Defense of Marriage Act makes no sense. It is a waste of time, energy, and money while the economy is going to Hell in a hurry. Sooner or later a dozen states will recognize same-sex marriage or civil unions. Under the "full faith and credit" clause of the Constitution, a *bona fide* marriage in Massachusetts or Connecticut will be recognized in all 50 states. It is only a matter of time that laws against same-sex marriage will be struck down as unconstitutional. No other decision makes any sense under the Constitution. But why should you care? No one is **making you** do anything. If not for bigotry and prejudice, why even discuss this subject, much less propose or support legislation to prevent it.

There is no one out there who is publicly "Pro-Abortion", "Against Immigration Reform", or "Anti-Gay." It is time we realize the end is coming and when it comes, our petty prejudices won't matter a damn bit. Just like a Yankee fan pinned down by enemy fire welcomes a platoon of Texas Rangers or even Red Sox fans coming over the ridge, and a Dallas Cowboy will gladly give blood to save the life of a New York Giant, so, too, will we welcome our fellow Americans when they come to help us in our time of need, be they Black, White, Hispanic, Asian, Middle-Eastern, Straight or Gay.

The asteroid's name is Wormwood. Read the Bible for yourself. Check it out and lighten up, before it is too late.

XXIX. Asteroids and the Mayan Calendar Part II It's the End of the World As We Know It

By now it should be obvious that if an asteroid can take out the dinosaurs, it can certainly end the World as we know it. T. Rex did not make Noah's Ark because he became extinct 60 million years earlier. This is not God versus Darwin. There is no need to revisit the Scopes trial. God exists and so do killer asteroids. Dinosaurs once ruled the Earth, and they were destroyed by an asteroid that struck Mexico. Let us all stop worrying about immigrants from Mexico, and start focusing on a real problem: the end of the World caused by a large asteroid hitting the Earth. And whether it hits Mexico, Brazil, Africa, or Russia – we will be destroyed just as the dinosaurs were. Yes – it will finally be true to say that we will be dead as the proverbial dinosaur – killed by the same cosmic criminal.

The President wants NASA to refocus and waste billions of dollars on landing a man on Mars by 2035 – and getting him back, of course. With all due respect to the President, H.G. Wells, and Orson Welles, you do not see anyone on Mars looking to spend $50 billion to come visit us. Once again, if the Mayans turn out to be correct – something catastrophic will be happening in December 2012; and no one will care who won the election of 2012.

Remember, the Mayans with their "primitive" culture could not only predict an eclipse and exactly when it would happen, but they could also predict the best place in the World to view that celestial spectacle a thousand years before it was to happen – and that viewing point was not in their backyard. We are not talking about the Freemasons designing a new capital city in Washington, D.C., we are talking about an ancient culture traveling thousands of miles to a remote island and sculpting a statue into a mountain as a tribute to, and a viewing stand for, their gods and ancestors. You would have a tough time finding this island on a map, much less getting a boat to take you there despite all of the travel services available today.

Also remember that the Bible makes no mention of the "Rapture", but clearly gives the name "Wormwood" to a killer asteroid, meteor, or comet. Not even the Antichrist can save us if a killer asteroid finds us first. That is why it is so interesting that in 2004, astronomers discovered a killer asteroid that narrowly missed us. In cosmic terms a narrow miss can be determined as one where the asteroid comes between the orbit of the Earth and the Moon, or roughly 242,000 miles from Earth. We had a number of near misses in 2010 – but because the asteroids were the size of a car or a bus or even a house, no one really cared. But in 2004, we discovered a near miss by a killer asteroid – after it had just missed us. We know that the asteroid, appropriately named Apophis, or "the Destroyer" – based on the Egyptian serpent god that ruled the skies and was beaten every morning by the God Ra – is scheduled to return several times between now and 2029. But it is specifically the 2029 return visit that is troubling to astronomers and scientists. On that return trip, Apophis could make a direct hit on Earth by being only one or two degrees off from its projected path.

Apophis is the classic killer asteroid, weighing in at 25 million tons, 800 feet wide, and traveling at 26,000 miles per hour. If and when it hits the Earth – supposedly on Friday the 13th of April 2029 – it will immediately destroy the country that it hits, or create a world-record Tsunami. It is the aftermath of the hit that will end life on Earth as we know it. Just as if we released all of the nuclear weapons in our arsenal – whether it was 20,000 or 50,000 atomic bombs like the one that destroyed Hiroshima – that much destruction, wherever it hit, would create a nuclear winter that would last long enough to kill everything on Earth (except for certain insects, microbes and lower life forms that thrive in cold, dark places).

Scientists, and even student Astronomers at places like the University of Alaska at Anchorage, are getting better and better at tracking asteroids. NASA has been brushing the dust off of its old playbooks for its "Deep Impact" program. The total cost that astronomers and scientists estimate it would take to track all of the potential "killer" asteroids is $150 million. That is the same amount that Exxon received back on its tax refund in 2009 for not paying taxes in the United States.

Instead of sending a man to Mars at a cost of $50 billion, the total cost for an effective anti-asteroid project to save the World would be about $5 billion, and even in its November 7, 2006 issue, Popular Mechanics Magazine had several ideas about how to knock a potentially hazardous asteroid off course.

Therefore, if we can all come together to support the victims of an earthquake in Haiti, or to stop the spread of malaria in Africa, or polio in India, should we not make the effort to begin a truly worthwhile project of funding an asteroid detection program at various state universities, and to direct NASA to come up with a program that will work when the killer asteroid is on its way? Asteroids of various sizes and shapes enter our atmosphere all the time with some very large ones hitting every hundred years or so. There is no question that we will be hit. It is only a question of "when" we will be hit – not "if" we will be hit – and by what size asteroid. It is only a matter of time before our luck runs out. Whether in 2012 or 2029, now is the time to get serious about the issues that really matter, and forget about the issues and causes that divide us.

The purpose of this Book is to suggest that America would be better off worrying about its own future economy and the well-being of its own citizens than to police the rest of the World at a cost it can no longer afford. Is it not better for America to be known for saving the miners in Chile, rather than killing innocent Pakistanis with attacks from unmanned drones? If we do not come to grips with our own national debt of future promises to pay of over $70 TRILLION, we will wish that the Mayans were right and that Wormwood does hit us in 2012. As much as we might want to, we cannot all move to Bermuda and start a new life as many of our corporate citizens have. Someone has to stay behind and take care of the America that the Founders dreamed of and fought for. If it is not you and us, and not now, then who will save America, and when?

Last but not least, it is important that the Republican Party return to its Jeffersonian roots – look it up if you don't believe us. That government is best, which governs least. The Constitution was meant to protect the people, we the people, the citizens, from an overly-intrusive and all-powerful government; not to protect the all-powerful government from its citizens. We all need to be like Jefferson: fiscally conservative, tough on defense, but liberal and compassionate in our thinking. If the Mayans are right, you do not have any time to waste thinking about abortion, gay marriage, or "don't ask, don't tell" policies in the military. When Wormwood or Apophis hits, it will cleanse the Earth of all the hatred, bigotry, and hypocrisy that we have built up over time ("where the grapes of wrath are stored") – so let us join together to do it now and address the issues that are truly important to America's future and our own, before it is too late.

www.ingramcontent.com/pod-product-compliance
Lightning Source LLC
Chambersburg PA
CBHW020419290526
45785CB00002B/629